turning the world upside down

D1350147

turning the world upside down

ROY CLEMENTS

inter-varsity press

INTER-VARSITY PRESS
38 De Montfort Street, Leicester LE1 7GP, England

First published under the title The church that turned the world upside down
by Crossway Books, Cambridge, in 1992

This edition 1998

British Library Cataloguing in Publication Data
A catalogue record for this book is available from the British Library.

ISBN 0-85110-897-0

Typeset in Great Britain by Nuprint Ltd, Station Road, Harpenden,
Herts AL5 4SE

Printed in Great Britain by Cox & Wyman Ltd, Reading,
Berkshire.

*Inter-Varsity Press is the book-publishing division of the Universities and
Colleges Christian Fellowship (formerly the Inter-Varsity Fellowship), a
student movement linking Christian Unions in universities and colleges
throughout the United Kingdom and the Republic of Ireland, and a member
movement of the International Fellowship of Evangelical Students. For
information about local and national activities write to UCCF, 38 De Montfort
Street, Leicester LE1 7GP.*

Contents

Acknowledgements

Much of the material for this book began as the Arthur DeMoss Memorial Lectures delivered at the Church of the Saviour in Wayne, Pennsylvania, during the year 1980. My thanks are due to Dr Bill Hogan, a valued friend and fellow enthusiast for biblical exposition, who invited me to give those lectures and encouraged their subsequent publication.

A debt of gratitude is also owed to Pat Blake for much hard work in preparing the manuscripts for publication and to Paul Riddington for assistance in editing them.

Roy Clements

Foreword

It is always an encouragement when you find a distinguished expositor who clearly agrees with yourself. I found Roy Clements' comments on Gamaliel very close to my own thinking and often at variance with commentators. Roy speaks of him as nailing his colours to the fence and indulging in vacillating compromise. It is always a dangerous attitude of mind and one which this book will do much to dispel. It is hard to come to a dynamic book like the Acts of the Apostles and remain agnostic.

The story of the church that turned the world upside down is a vivid description of a group of people with so vital a living faith that it produced testimony to the fact that they had indeed turned the world upside down, or was it the right way up? Equally the church itself was turned inside out by the working of the Spirit. We desperately need such a transformation in the church of our day. There is no better way for this to happen than for us to turn to the early chapters of Acts with the help of this exposition.

It is vital to remind ourselves that Acts is not a blue-print for the church of our day. We may not expect God to work in exactly the same way as he did in those early days of the church. But Acts is a reminder of the foundation documents of the church's life. There is no diminution of the power of God, and he can be similarly at work in our day. A close reading of these chapters may make some people want to be like Gamaliel, for it is a costly business to be in that kind of a church. Ask Ananias and Sapphira.

Luke begins his second volume with a reminder that his Gospel is a story of all that Jesus began to do and teach. This narrative is the story of the continuing work of Jesus, and that work still continues. It is urgent that we relate these early days of the church's growth and life to the world of today. This book will help us enormously. Bible exposition needs to be earthed in two ways so that it can effectively convey God's truth to people. It must be earthed clearly and unequivocally in the authority of Scripture as once for all given to us. Equally it must be earthed in the world of today. In Roy Clements' individual style of exposition this is clearly accomplished. As well as the references to our contemporary situation, the whole ethos of the book is directly relevant to today's world.

Acts 1:8 is always seen as an index to the contents of this remarkable book. In these pages we go to a particular climax of the story, with the first overseas missionary venture springing out from the new church in Antioch. In one sense the church was therefore already beginning to reach the ends of the earth. By the end of Acts the gospel was being proclaimed in Rome, at the very heart of the world of that day. But there will be no final accomplishment of the task until the day of our Lord's return. Into that unfinished task we must go with renewed conviction in the power of God's Word and the enabling of God's Spirit. With Word and Spirit working together we can at least hope to see in our generation that task becoming less unfinished. We can then hand on to the next generation a better foundation and springboard for action than is evident at this moment. Perhaps the Gamaliel spirit is still abroad in the church. My prayer is that this book will transform some Gamaliels into Pauls.

Philip Hacking

1

The Butterfly Effect

Acts 1:1—2:41

'But you will receive power when the Holy Spirit comes on you; and you will be my witnesses in Jerusalem, and in all Judea and Samaria, and to the ends of the earth.'

Now there were staying in Jerusalem God fearing Jews from every nation under heaven. When they heard this sound, a crowd came together in bewilderment, because each one heard them speaking in his own language.

Acts 1:7–8; 2:5–7

EDWARD LORENZ was a physicist, working in the Massachusetts Institute of Technology in the 1960s on the computer—modelling of weather systems. He devised a program which, once he had typed in certain meteorological observations, could calculate, at least in theory, what the subsequent weather pattern was going to be. One day he made a mistake. He had intended to type into the computer a piece of data consisting of six decimal places, 0.506127, but he accidentally inserted only the first three digits, 0.506.

He was a thorough researcher and decided he ought to run the program again with the correct number in place, although intuition assured him that such a small error, only one part in one thousand, could not possibly change the results significantly. To his amazement, however, when the computer plotted out the revised weather pattern, it was completely different from the earlier graph. Lorenz could not believe his eyes. As he later explained, it was just as if a tiny atmospheric disturbance in Peking, no greater than the beat of a butterfly's wing should a week or so later give rise to a force twelve hurricane in New York.

11

Hence the name of his discovery: 'The Butterfly Effect'. It has aroused a great deal of scientific interest in recent years. Among other things, it explains why our weather forecasters get it wrong so often. It is not their fault; blame it on the butterflies in Peking which the satellite did not pick up. Such is the complexity of the earth's atmosphere that even tiny unobservable disturbances can generate momentous meteoroligcal consequences and thus render precise long-range weather forecasting not just difficult, but theoretically impossible.

Fortunately, life in general is not vulnerable to such chaotic 'Butterfly Effect' fluctuations. It is just as well, or we would never be able to plan anything with any degree of reliability. But in some respects it is rather depressing too, for it means it is difficult to change the world. It is true that every decision we take does make some difference and that every one of us has the potential to alter the course of events in minor ways. But in the main such individual actions on our part are a bit like stones tossed into a very large lake. They cause a splash, but usually the ripples die away very quickly and are not even perceptible beyond the very local area in which the stone fell. There is no 'Butterfly Effect' magnifying the little contribution we make into something more significant.

Jonathan Swift gave it as his opinion that whoever could make two ears of corn grow upon a spot of ground, where only one ear grew before, had accomplished more in his lifetime than the whole race of politicians put together. Sadly, even so modest a contribution to the long-term future of the human race is a rare achievement. Most of us have to face the fact that we shall drop the little pebble of our lives into the turbulent ocean of world events and in no time at all the surface will bear no trace of our passing. Indeed, for many this is the chief anxiety of modern men and women. The futility of existence has been the theme of countless contemporary novels and plays.

However, the situation is not totally bleak. Just occasionally the 'Butterfly Effect' seems to work in other situations too. Do you remember this children's rhyme for instance?

> For want of a nail the shoe was lost
> For want of a shoe the horse was lost
> For want of a horse the rider was lost
> For want of a rider the battle was lost
> For want of a battle the kingdom was lost

A single nail on rare occasions, it seems, can be the difference between victory and defeat for an entire nation. And what goes for single nails can sometimes go for single lives also.

He was born in an obscure village, the child of a peasant woman.
He grew up in still another village where he worked in a carpenter's shop till he was thirty.
Then for three years he was an itinerant preacher.
He never wrote a book.
He never held an office.
He never had a family.
He never owned a house.
He did not go to college.
He never travelled more than 200 miles from the place where he was born.
He did not do any of the things one usually associates with greatness.

He was only thirty-three when the tide of public
   opinion turned against him.
His friends ran away.
He was turned over to his enemies.
He went through a mockery of a trial.
He was nailed to a cross between two thieves while
   the executioners gambled for his clothing, the only
   property he had on earth.
And when he was dead he was laid in a borrowed
   grave.
Nineteen centuries have come and gone but the world
   is still enthralled by him.
All the armies that ever marched.
All the navies that ever sailed.
All the parliaments that ever sat.
All the kings that ever reigned.
Put together, have no affected the life of man on this
   earth
As much as that ONE SOLITARY LIFE.

It is the 'Butterfly Effect' you see, operating this time
not in meteorology but in history. The ripples of this
'one solitary life' did not die away at death. On the
contrary, the effects of Jesus' coming have increased
in amplitude and expanded in diameter, until they
have become great tidal waves encompassing the
entire globe.

In this book, we are going to be studying a part of
the Bible which has a special interest in mapping the
progress of those ever-increasing circles of Jesus'
influence: the Acts of the Apostles. Acts is in fact the
second part of a two-volume treatise. We know the
first part as the Gospel of Luke. Both parts are dedicated to the same man, Theophilus. He may well
have been a Roman aristocrat, for Luke, the author,
addresses him as 'Your Excellency'. Luke writes then

in order to inform an educated Gentile of the extra-ordinary and growing effect of Christianity on the world. And Acts is a further contribution towards that goal: 'In my former book, Theophilus, I wrote about all that Jesus began to do and to teach' (1:1).

Notice the word 'began'. In his Gospel, Luke has told us how Jesus was born in an obscure village to a peasant woman. He has told us how he grew up in the humble home of Joseph the carpenter. He has recounted his short adult ministry, which though supernatural was confined within the boundaries of Judea and its neighbouring provinces. Finally, he has described his ignominious death, and his glorious resurrection. At the end of the Gospel of Luke, Jesus returns to heaven. You would have thought that the story was over. 'On the contrary,' says Luke, 'that is only the end of the beginning. There is much more to come yet.'

The story of this one solitary life did not end with death. Jesus is still doing things in the world and having a more and more conspicuous effect upon human history as the circles of his influence spread further and further afield. Indeed, he is not going to be satisfied until those ever-increasing circles have embraced the four corners of the world.

> They asked him, 'Lord, are you at this time going to restore the kingdom to Israel?' He said to them: 'It is not for you to know the times or dates the Father has set by his own authority. But you will receive power when the Holy Spirit comes on you; and you will be my witnesses in Jerusalem, and in all Judea and Samaria, and to the ends of the earth' (1:6–7).

These verses constitute the agenda of the whole Book

of Acts. Notice the two implicit rebukes to the disciples which they contain, and the very explicit promise. The first rebuke concerns their *inquisitiveness*. Clearly, Jesus had been explaining to them how, with his coming, the messianic age had dawned and the ancient prophecies were being fulfilled. This inevitably set his disciples' thoughts in motion about the nearness of the end of the world. Immediately, Jesus cautions them against such speculations. Information of that sort, he insists, is in a drawer marked 'Top Secret' in God's private vault. There are certain things you are not meant to know, and that is one of them.

There are still some Christians, of course, who are obsessed with dates and times. The tiniest political incident in the Middle East is sufficient to send them off into feverish analysis of the Book of Daniel with their pocket calculators at the ready. We need to beware of that kind of hysteria today as they did then. 'You are not here to make guesses about dates and times,' Jesus says in effect. 'You are here to multiply so that when I return at the end of the age, I have a kingdom to return to. Evangelism is to be your first priority.'

Secondly, he rebukes them for their *parochialism*. They enquire about 'Israel', but he replies in terms of 'the ends of the earth'. Their minds are clearly focused around the destiny of their own nation. In spite of all Jesus' teaching, their ideas of the kingdom of God are still fundamentally chauvinistic and territorial. They have yet to understand the 'Butterfly Effect'. 'Listen,' says Jesus, 'the ripples which my death and resurrection have set in motion must expand: first here in Jerusalem, but then in Judea and Samaria and finally to the ends of the earth. And you, my disciples, are going to play a key role in that expansion process. You will be my *witnesses*.'

The Book of Acts is, in many ways, simply the record of the fulfilment of that agenda. It chronicles how the apostles did indeed take the news of Jesus' resurrection to the world, so that instead of his influence petering out after his departure, it grew greater and greater until the 'Butterfly Effect' of his life sent waves battering on the very capital of the ancient world itself. But clearly, here in chapter 1, they were not yet ready for that. They were far too parochial in their mentality to see themselves as world-changing missionaries. Something else was needed, something pretty dramatic, and Jesus knew what it was. Hence he couples his rebukes with a promise: 'You will receive power when the Holy Spirit comes on you' (1:8).

It is the power of the sun which drives the 'Butterfly Effect' in weather systems. It is only because the sun heats the earth's atmosphere, creating enormous turbulence, that minor atmospheric disturbances can be transformed into major cyclonic convulsions. Every physicist knows you cannot make waves without energy. Similarly, Jesus here identifies for us the energy source which would drive the 'Butterfly Effect' in church history, transforming what was initially no more than a minor Jewish sect into a major world faith. Luke goes on in chapter 2 to recount for us the moment when that 'power' supply was switched on and the ripples began to spread.

When the day of Pentecost came, they were all together in one place. Suddenly a sound like the blowing of a violent wind came from heaven and filled the whole house where they were sitting. They saw what seemed to be tongues of fire that separated and came to rest on each of them. All of them were filled with the Holy Spirit and began to speak in other tongues as the Spirit enabled them (2:1–4).

In the Old Testament, Pentecost was a harvest festival. But by the time of Jesus, it had an additional significance in the Jewish calendar. It was the time at which they commemorated the giving of the Ten Commandments. That association may well be significant here, for the violent wind and tongues of flame which we read about are reminiscent of the storm and the lightning which enveloped Moses on Mount Sinai. He received there the law of the Old Covenant carved in tablets of stone: the law which would have been read in public on the Day of Pentecost in Jerusalem. But as the prophets of the Old Testament had many times explained, that law had failed to change the world because it had failed to change people.

Now, once again, God was coming down at Pentecost in fire and wind. But not this time to impart the law; rather to bestow his Spirit, and thus initiate the *New* Covenant, written not on lifeless tablets of stone, but on renewed human hearts. The Spirit would succeed where the law had failed, bringing not just commands from God, but power. Here was the dynamic that would amplify the butterfly-like wing beats of twelve unimpressive Galilean peasants and turn their testimony into a revolutionary tide that would transform the moral and social values of human civilisation.

And in the miracle that accompanied the Spirit's arrival, God signals how he intends to achieve that transformation in a very interesting way. He makes

clear that the Spirit will dismantle the social alienations that divide the world. He will prove himself a
power that breaks down barriers. Ripples cannot
spread if they hit a brick wall, and there were many
such obstructions in the ancient world which would
have to be overcome if Jesus' ambition of world
conquest was to be achieved. And the Spirit had the
energy to demolish them.

> There were staying in Jerusalem God-fearing Jews
> from every nation under heaven. When they heard this
> sound, a crowd came together in bewilderment,
> because each one heard them speaking in his own
> language. Utterly amazed, they asked: 'Are not all
> these men who are speaking Galileans? Then how is it
> that each of us hears them in his own native
> language?' (2:5–8).

One of the things that recent liberalisation policies
in the Soviet Union have made very clear, is the
resilient tenacity of nationalism. No matter how
ruthlessly an empire such as that of Stalin sought to
pacify its subject peoples, ethnic loyalties survived.
The military intimidation had only to be relaxed a
fraction, and independence movements started
sprouting in all directions, just as if half a century of
repression had never happened. The reason for that,
of course, is quite simple; nationhood is not fundamentally a function of political organisation. It is a
cultural phenomenon. A people may lose its political
self-determination for many centuries and yet still
retain a most vigorous sense of national identity by
virtue of its cultural distinctives. Things like the
clothes we wear, the music we play, the folk tales we
teach our children in bed at night, and perhaps most

19

distinctive of all, the language we speak; these are labels by which national identity is preserved. They enable us to recognise a foreigner immediately. And they constitute a formidable obstacle for any movement which wants to unify the divided peoples of the world. Mere political integration is not enough. The real challenge is that of *cultural* integration.

The usual way in which governments have tried to make people 'one' is by forcing them all to be the same. A single dominant culture is imposed over the top of indigenous cultures.

Islam, for example, claims to generate a genuine internationalism, but makes it very clear that this can only be achieved by the dominance of Arabic culture. The Arabic language is absolutely central to Islam and every Muslim must learn it. But the conflicts we have seen in the Gulf in past years have proved beyond doubt, if we need any proof, that nationalist rivalry still persists in spite of this.

Similarly, the Leninist dream of creating a world-wide classless society hinged on the repression of those who refused to conform to its stereotype image of a socialist man. The disintegration of the Eastern bloc has only emphasised the persistence of national rivalry in spite of nearly a century of such Soviet 'union'. Nor should we forget that the ambition of nineteenth-century colonialism to unite the world in one great empire envisaged, of course, a *British* empire. And this too has failed to resist the inexorable assertion of tribalistic and nationalistic independence movements.

The trouble with all the methods by which we seek to create a single world order is that they are implicitly imperialistic, involving the domination of one culture over another. And culture refuses to be eliminated in that way. It survives no matter how repressive the regime. In fact, it even thrives on persecution. This is the problem of Northern Ireland; it is not fundamentally a conflict between two political parties, or even two religions; it is two cultures that are in collision there.

Those of us who know our Bibles ought not to be surprised at all this. It is the lesson of Babel. The Book of Genesis tells us how it was God himself who divided mankind into rival nationalities, because amazingly we are much less dangerous that way. To try to unify the world by a means of cultural imperialism, and thus erode the national diversity of the human race, is therefore bound to fail, since it flies in the face of that ancient Babel decree.

Is there a power that can unify the divided nations of the earth without subjugating them in the process? Is there a way of making people one, without at the same time making them all the same? I suggest to you that there is. It is precisely that sort of unity which the Holy Spirit brings. And he declared his intention in the matter right at the beginning, on the Day of Pentecost, by the miracle he performed: 'Utterly amazed, they asked: 'Are not all these men who are speaking Galileans? Then how is it that each of us hears them in his own native language?'' (2:7–8).

God could have given this crowd a universal tongue. He could have enabled them all to understand one language, but he did not need to do that because they already understood such a language, namely Greek. There would have been little difficulty for Peter to make himself understood in Greek; indeed most if not all early Christian preaching was conducted in it. The sign of tongues was not necessitated, then, by the lack of bilingual interpreters.

The point is, as Luke carefully tells us, that all these crowds who had gathered from so many different places, heard the message as if it was being spoken in their own *vernacular*. That is the very word they used. 'Each of us hears...in his own native language' (v 8) or, literally, *dialect*. For a moment the notoriously heavy Galilean accent of the disciples had disappeared and each member of the audience heard the praise of God as if it were coming from the lips of one of their own group, living in their local area back home. That is what startled them. They could have understood the disciples in Greek, but instead each person in the crowd heard them not as foreigners but as if they were members of their own clan or tribe or nation.

These pentecostal tongues were a pointer to the way in which the Holy Spirit was going to break down social barriers and create an unprecedented kind of internationalism. Unlike the imperialisms of men, the Spirit had no ambition to homogenise the peoples of the world into a uniform Christian culture. On the contrary, he intended to bridge cultures and to overcome the alienation they create without eroding the diversity they represent. The Jew would be a Jew still and the Greek would be a Greek still. The dividing walls of culture would not be destroyed, but lowered to the point of innocuousness, being superseded by a new kind of social identity altogether. So distinctive would it be that they would coin a new word to describe it—'the *fellowship* of the Holy Spirit'. Here there would be 'neither Jew nor Greek, slave nor free, male nor female, for you are all one in Christ Jesus' (Gal 3:28).

At Pentecost the disciples preached *one* message which was heard in diverse tongues. As we read the

Book of Acts, we shall discover that message produced *one* church in diverse cultures. If we looked further into the Book of Revelation we should find ultimately it produces *one* multitude gathered around the throne of God from every tribe and nation and kindred, and recognisably so. Their ethnic origins are not effaced in glory; there will be *one* community representing the whole range of human culture, praising one multi-lingual God. That is the Bible's vision of eternity. That is what the Holy Spirit intends to create, and those are the kinds of waves which he began to send through the world on the Day of Pentecost.

This has all kinds of implications for us. At a fairly trivial level, it is what makes translations of the Bible acceptable. We probably take our English Bible for granted, but there are many religions in the world that have great torments of conscience about translating their Holy Scripture: the Koran can only be authentically heard in Arabic; the Vedic Scriptures of India can only be authentically studied in Sanskrit. Some orthodox Jews have a very superstitious regard for the Hebrew text of the Old Testament. And Christianity itself has not been immune from this kind of linguistic elitism over the centuries. There was a time when the Roman church insisted that the scripture and liturgy of the church had to be in Latin. And you still come across some Protestants who feel there is some special sanctity about the language of sixteenth- and seventeenth-century England. But all such attempts to link the gospel to some special holy language are an offence against the Spirit of Pentecost. The Holy Spirit, on the first day of the church's missionary expansion, made it clear that *every* language is an appropriate vehicle for the praise of Jesus

Christ. That is why Tyndale was right to render the New Testament into the ordinary speech of the men and women of his day. That is why Wycliffe Bible Translators are right today to try to translate the Scriptures into the local languages of every tribe on earth. This is the ambition of the Holy Spirit. He wants people to know that this message is distinctively their own. He does not require of them any surrender of their identity. No, Jesus is for them, for their nation, for their people.

The sign of Pentecost is also, more generally, a warning against the very great danger of tying the presentation of the gospel that we give to the world to our own culture. The early Christians, I am afraid, took some time to understand this. Being fiercely patriotic Jews, it is understandable that they should feel that anybody who wanted to become a Christian must become at least a little bit Jewish. Some argued that Gentile converts should be circumcised, observe kosher food laws and keep the Sabbath, for instance. The early church had to think very carefully about this matter, for these cultural distinctives were so deeply ingrained in Jewish consciousness that it was almost impossible for Jews to welcome as equals, into the people of God, those who did not submit to them. But eventually, the Holy Spirit had his way. What we find in the Book of Acts is the very remarkable story of how a group of immensely chauvinistic Jews broke out of the cultural box of their parent Judaism and began to baptise into one church of Jesus Christ, first Samaritans, and eventually uncircumcised Gentiles. Right from the very beginning, the sign of Pentecost pointed them in this direction. By his strange gift the Holy Spirit indicated that Christ is not the possession of any specific culture. In the years since, we have not always recognised the importance of this. Sometimes, when Western missionaries have gone out, they have tried to plant churches which are just like the ones back home— even to the extent that they sing the same hymn tunes and use the same architecture. Sometimes they even wear the same Sunday suits and bonnets. This is just a Christianised form of cultural imperialism. It is a most fundamental mistake for it offends against the Spirit of pentecostal diversity.

Finally, the sign of Pentecost also has very profound implications regarding the kind of church we ought to seek to be today. Some theorists of church growth argue very strongly that each local congregation should target a particular type of person, because sociological evidence shows that such homogenous cultural groups are most effective in evangelising other people from a similar background. Chinese churches are best at reaching Chinese people. West Indian churches are most effective at reaching the Caribbean community. Middle class churches are best for yuppies. Working class churches are best for council estates, and so on. It is impossible to contradict statistical evidence in favour of such a policy.

Yet for all that we recognise the sociological wisdom in saying that homogenous groups are the most evangelistically effective, it really is contrary to the Spirit of Pentecost to build the church in such a culturally discriminating fashion. The goal of the church of Jesus Christ must be integration; never segregation. Whatever the church growth gains may be, the Holy Spirit cannot possibly sanctify ecclesiastical apartheid. While it may be expedient for evangelistic purposes to have house fellowships,

Bible-study groups and so on which do have a homogenous population, or which target specialised groups in the community, the goal of such groups and fellowships must be to bring those who are won from the world into the *one* church of Jesus Christ. It is the glory of the church that it is a technicolour institution comprising black and white, educated and illiterate, young and old. No other institution on earth achieves such a cultural integration. But then no other institution on earth has the gale of the Holy Spirit driving it along.

Such unity is not achieved without difficulty. It requires sensitivity and understanding. But these are the very qualities the Holy Spirit engenders. He seeks a unity without uniformity. It is his distinctive mark. When God freezes the water, he makes a snow storm in which every flake is different. When we human beings freeze water, we make ice cubes! The Holy Spirit wants to make us a people who rejoice in our differences, just as the disciples rejoiced to proclaim Christ in different languages on the Day of Pentecost. It was a sign that the church of Jesus Christ is not intended to exhibit the martial unison of regimental khaki, but the multi-tonal harmony of a symphony orchestra.

God intends the good news of Jesus Christ to captivate hearts in every nation. The ripples began to spread on that Day of Pentecost, and they continue to spread wherever Christian disciples testify to the good news of Jesus with no culturally imperialistic strings attached. We don't have to fear that our lives will be wasted when empowered by his Spirit. No matter how apparently insignificant, they can make a world-changing contribution to those ever-increasing circles. The 'Butterfly Effect' can magnify the impact of our lives as it magnified the testimony of the early church. According to Jesus, even the 'gates of hell' are no match for the tidal power of his church.

2

The New Society

Acts 2:42−47

They devoted themselves to the apostles'
teaching and to the fellowship, to the
breaking of bread and to prayer.
Everyone was filled with awe, and many
wonders and miraculous signs were done
by the apostles. All the believers were
together and had everything in common.
Selling their possessions and goods, they
gave to anyone as he had need. Every day
they continued to meet together in the
temple courts. They broke bread in their
homes and ate together with glad and
sincere hearts praising God and enjoying
the favour of all the people. And the Lord
added to their number daily those who
were being saved...

Acts 2:42−47

I BELIEVE that the quality of community in our Western society has declined in recent years. That decline is evidenced in the prevalence of anxiety and depression in the population, and in the escalating statistics of divorce, suicide, drug abuse and juvenile crime. But most of all, it shows in the superficiality of our personal relationships.

Eric Fromm writes in his book *The Sane Society*: 'There is not much love to be found in the world of our day. There is rather a superficial friendliness concealing a distance, an indifference, a subtle distrust.' R. D. Laing, the radical psychiatrist, in his book *The Politics of Experience* goes further when he writes: 'We are born into a world where social alienation awaits us. Before we can even ask such optimistic questions as 'What is a personal relationship?' we have to ask if personal relationships are even possible in our present situation.' Karen Horney, another respected psychiatrist, affirms in her book *The Neurotic Personality of Our Time*: 'The average individual today, even when he has many contacts with others and is happily married, nevertheless feels comparatively emotionally isolated. He is caught in the dilemma of hungering for a great deal of affection, and yet finding great difficulty in obtaining it.' But perhaps the most penetrating comments of all on the subject are to be found in *The Culture of Narcissism* by Christopher Lasch:

> Our society has made lasting friendships, love affairs and marriages increasingly difficult to achieve. Social life has become more and more war-like and personal relationships have taken on the character of combat. Some dignify the combat, offering courses in assertiveness training. Others celebrate the impermanent attachments that result, with slogans like 'open marriage', but in doing so they merely intensify the pervasive dissatisfaction with the quality of human relationships which is at the heart of our problem.

I do not know if those phrases 'superficial friendliness', 'emotional isolation' and 'social alienation' ring true in your experience, but they certainly do in mine. As a pastoral counsellor, I am sure Lasch is correct when he speaks of a 'pervasive dissatisfaction with the quality of human relationships' in our world today. It seems that the rise of individualism in our Western society means that we no longer think of human relationships as the fundamental stuff of which life is composed. On the contrary, *self*-fulfilment is our watchword today. If relationships are important at all, it is simply as a means to that egocentric end.

Eric Fromm blames the capitalist system, R. D. Laing the emotional suffocation of the nuclear family and Karen Horney attributes it to the rivalry and acquisitiveness of consumerism. Christopher Lasch is to my mind closest to the truth when he links his observation of narcissistic behaviour to the decay of religious faith and the loss of confidence in the future. But although their perspectives differ on the precise cause of this social malaise, all these writers are unanimous in their diagnosis of the sick society we have created. Our contemporary world desperately needs to rediscover the meaning of *community*. That sense of mutual care and mutual involvement which derives from the consciousness that in some very profound and experiential way we belong to one another. Few of us enjoy that sense of corporate identity today.

There is however a sign of hope. The opening chapters of Acts point us to the place where such community ought to be found. It is quite clear from the end of chapter 2 that in Luke's mind a Christian is not an individualist who enjoys a private relationship with God, but a member of a new society, inescapably bound up with every other Christian in a mutual solidarity of a very special kind.

Sometimes they called it the 'body of Christ', sometimes the 'fellowship of the Holy Spirit'. Most frequently they simply referred to 'the church'. All these expressions refer to the new community to which Christian believers found they belonged, and which played a vital part in propagating those everincreasing circles of influence through the world.

The sign of membership

When the people heard this, they were cut to the heart and said to Peter and the other apostles, 'Brothers, what shall we do?' Peter replied, 'Repent and be baptised, every one of you, in the name of Jesus Christ so that your sins may be forgiven. And you will receive the gift of the Holy Spirit' (Acts 2:37–38).

Some people are embarrassed by the almost casual connection that Peter seems to imply in these verses between baptism and salvation. 'Be baptised' he says, 'and you will receive the gift of the Holy Spirit' (v 38), as if he believed the grace of God was mediated by water. There are, of course, some sacramentalists who would argue that was exactly what he did believe, but I do not think the rest of the New Testament lends much support to such a view. What is clear, however, from the close link these verses establish between baptism and salvation, is that for the early church, to be a Christian believer and to be a baptised member of the church were practically synonymous. I doubt whether an early Christian could have distinguished between the two, for baptism was the universal sign of faith: 'Be baptised, every one of you' (v 38). There were no exceptions and there was no delay.

We have lost the immediacy of that connection between faith and baptism today. Partly, it is the result of infant baptism which has given rise to something that the New Testament does not anticipate, namely a *baptised unbeliever*. In part too it is the result of evangelism conducted by para-church organisations, which do not practise baptism for understandable reasons of inter-church politics. That has also given rise to something the New Testament never anticipated, namely an *unbaptised believer*.

I suspect, however, that the major reason for the detachment of baptism from faith—and its consequent displacement from the important place it clearly had in the conversion experience of first-century Christians—is more fundamental still. It lies in the fact that we have a view of salvation subtly different from theirs. True to our cultural origins, we think of salvation as individualistic, something we each experience on our own. But for the early Christians, salvation was much more a matter of leaving a community under judgement, to find refuge in the saved community of the church. Notice how the text puts it:

> With many other words he warned them; and he pleaded with them, 'Save yourselves from this corrupt generation.' Those who accepted his message were baptised, and about three thousand were added to their number that day. They devoted themselves to the apostles' teaching and to the fellowship (Acts 2:40–42).

It is quite true, of course, that an individual decision to repent was required, but it was a decision to leave one group, 'this corrupt generation', and join a new group, 'the fellowship'. We find this all through the New Testament. The experience of salvation is very much tied up with a sense of belonging to the covenant people of God. There was no such thing as a solitary Christian. To be a Christian was, by definition, to be known publicly as a member of the local church. And it was baptism which signified that new identity.

Augustine popularised the phrase 'Non salus extra ecclesiam' ('No salvation outside the church'). It was much abused in medieval church history, but rightly understood it is a true statement. For to be saved in the New Testament was to be a member of the *saved* community. You could not be a Christian without being automatically welded into that new community. It was part of the deal. How did you know who belonged to it? It was easy: they were the baptised ones. To Jews, familiar with the idea of a covenant people marked by circumcision, this was perfectly intelligible. It is only novel to us, I suspect, because we have been brain-washed by our Western individualism. Consequently, we see the church in the same lukewarm terms in which we see every other kind of community: namely as a voluntary club that we join if we want to, rather than as *the* people of God with whom we must identify if we would be Christians at all.

A Christian without a church is an anomaly and one whose spiritual experience is bound to be impoverished immeasurably as a result.

The experience of belonging

> They devoted themselves to the apostles' teaching and to the fellowship, to the breaking of bread and to prayer. Everyone was filled with awe, and many wonders and miraculous signs were done by the apostles (2:42–43).

Do you notice the very high degree of voluntary commitment which the believers displayed towards this new community of which they became a part? Verse 42 speaks of their 'devotion' to corporate activity. There is something movingly spontaneous about their desire to do things together. Here was a group of people who did not want to be spectators, but participants. Church for them was not just an institution they went to on a Sunday, it was a community that formed the context of their whole lives and about which they felt passionately enthusiastic.

Luke tells us first of all that they were committed to *learning* together: 'They devoted themselves to the apostles' teaching' (2:42). That word 'teaching' in other contexts might very easily be translated 'doctrine', a word that sends shudders down the spine, perhaps, of some of us. This new society was structured around an informed grasp of Christian truth. Notice that it is the apostles who do the teaching. That is important, for it sheds light upon Luke's additional observation that many wonders and miraculous signs were done by the apostles. The function of miracles, in the Bible, is often to accredit God's special messengers. That is why you find that miracles are not distributed evenly through the Bible, but occur in concentrated pockets linked to specially authoritative individuals, like Elijah, Jesus and the apostles.

I am not saying, of course, that apostles were the only ones who worked miracles in the early church. We know that there were more general gifts of healing too. Nor am I suggesting that miracles do not happen today, for clearly they do. But with the passing of the apostles, one of the major reasons for the supernatural signs which we read about in the Book of Acts has gone. The apostles were special, and these signs were designed to mark them out in the special office they exercised. So we are probably mistaken if we anticipate the same density of supernatural events in the church today as was characteristic of the church then.

It is important to notice that it was the apostles who did the teaching for a second reason. You do sometimes come across the idea that the early church was itself a theologically creative institution, which invented the story of Jesus and the resurrection and all that it meant out of its own genius. It is quite clear that Luke does not believe that is the right explanation of the origin of New Testament doctrine. On the contrary, he insists that from the very beginning, the apostles were the uniquely authorised definers of Christian faith and conduct. It was not the church that created the doctrine; the early church was taught its doctrine by those who had themselves been personally instructed by Christ. That, of course, is why the New Testament is so critically important to us. It is our record of the apostles' teaching. We can still 'devote ourselves to the apostles' teaching', even though the apostles are long since dead, by devoting ourselves to the study of the New Testament. Not the sharing of our own ideas, but disciplined Bible learning—this is to be the source of our 'teaching' today. Some people do complain that sermons are too long, but I tell you this: if we had anything like the spiritual appetite of those early Christians, we would never stop complaining that sermons are far too short.

Luke records also that they were committed to the *fellowship*. Notice again the intense sense of involvement that they display. That word 'fellowship' seems to be a blanket term for everything not embraced in the earlier word 'teaching'. So it probably includes the breaking of bread and prayer, which he goes on to describe. Breaking of bread is not just a reference to mutual hospitality. Almost certainly it is a reference to the celebration of the Lord's Supper, the memorial of Christ's death, which right from the beginning these early Christians observed.

Such fellowship times, you will notice, involved both public worship in the temple courts and much more informal occasions in private homes. The latter are particularly relevant for us today, for as we said earlier, many people are dissatisfied today with the quality of their personal relationships. Such relationships can only grow close and intimate when you are in a small group. As a member of a crowd numbering hundreds, or even thousands, of people, as these early Christians were in the temple courts, it is quite impossible to form close relationships with people. The individual feels lost in such large groups. While there is no doubt a certain exhilaration in being part of a great company of people singing God's praise, it is not in such encounters that we discover interpersonal intimacy. If we are really going to feel we belong, there has to be small group experience too. God has set us in families for this very reason— only in such a small circle can love become a meaningful word for us. Indeed, that is one of the major reasons the community life of the church is so critically important in the twentieth century. For families are increasingly breaking down, and people's emotional needs are often not met as a result. Keith Miller asserts:

> Churches today are filled with people who outwardly look contented and at peace, but are inwardly crying out for someone to love them. Confused, frustrated, guilty, often unable to communicate, even with their own families. But the problem is that other people they see in church look so happy and content and self-sufficient, they have never have the courage to admit their deepest needs.

We need to encourage people to step outside that social paralysis born of the inhibiting fear of rejection, so that they can discover warm, intimate personal relationships with others. And small groups are the key to such 'fellowship'.

A community that cares

> All the believers were together and had everything in common. Selling their possessions and goods, they gave to anyone as he had need (2:44–45).

This third aspect of their communal life has often been described as 'primitive communism', but I think that is a thoroughly misleading phrase to use for two main reasons.

First, it is not at all certain that the early church abolished private property. It seems closer to the truth that there was a renunciation of *possessiveness*: 'All the believers were one in heart and mind. No-one claimed that any of his possessions was his own, but they shared everything they had' (4:32). So liberal were they in the sharing of their material resources, that the question 'Who owns what?' seems to have become irrelevant. It was not an example of communistic theory, but simply of extraordinary generosity.

This is confirmed by the observation that where property transactions did take place in the early church, they were quite voluntary: 'There were no needy persons among them. For from time to time those who owned lands or houses sold them, brought the money from the sales and put it at the apostles' feet' (4:34).

It was not that the church collectively owned the land or the houses, but the individual owners chose to bring the money from the sales and put it at the disposal of the church leadership for the relief of the needy. Clearly, then, this was not some centrally organised exercise in distributive justice carried out by commissars Peter and John, but an exceptionally beautiful example of Christian charity.

Even though the phrase 'primitive communism' is not appropriate, we do nevertheless see here something which comes very close to the fulfilment of the Marxist dream: 'From each according to his abilities, to each according to his needs.' Yet it is fulfilled here without tanks, bureaucrats or labour camps. Marx was right about it requiring a revolution, but not the kind that comes from the barrel of a gun. This revolution came through a tongue of fire from heaven that transformed the hearts of these people. They were not sharing with one another because they had come to believe in dialectical materialism, but because they did not believe in materialism at all. There were no needy persons among them because the Holy Spirit had created a new kind of caring society among them.

This seems to me to be an aspect of the life of the early church which has very special relevance as we think about the way the ever-increasing circles of Christian influence permeate the world. One of the major concerns missiologists have had in recent years is the relationship between evangelism and social action. There are those who want to merge these into a common tool of Christian action that they call 'mission'. The clearest example of this was seen in the World Council of Churches in the sixties and seventies, where it often was argued that the purpose of Christian mission includes the emancipation of the coloured races, the economic development of the third world, the eradication of class divisions, the overcoming of industrial disputes, and so on.

At the other extreme are those who argue that Christian mission should simply be teaching the gospel and nothing else; medical work, education, agricultural development and famine relief are a dangerous side-track. If missionaries engage in such activities at all, then at the very best it is simply as bait for the evangelistic hook; the taste of honey on the evangelistic pill.

It seems to me that evidence from the early chapters of Acts counts directly against both these extremes. Clearly this was a church that had a social conscience. And its social programme was very much bound up in Luke's view with the rapidity of its growth. But there was no ulterior motive in their involvement in the relief of poverty. It was no manipulative stratagem to win adherents. On the contrary, it was a spontaneous expression of the love for one another which the Holy Spirit had poured into their hearts.

What is more, there is no evidence at all that the early church confused this ministry to people's material needs with the evangelistic task which Jesus had given them to do: 'With great power the apostles continued to testify to the resurrection of the Lord Jesus, and much grace was with them all' (4:33).

Luke sandwiches that statement in among his record of the church's social concern. Clearly, then, it was not a case of substituting social action for evangelism, or of merging social action with evangelism, but of preaching the love of God in Christ, in the context of a community that demonstrated that love practically. This combination of evangelistic preaching and social concern must characterise the agenda of a growing church today as well. The apostles were not content simply to win individual converts to faith. They insisted that this new caring community should always be the product of true evangelism.

Such a community, by its body life, gives indispensable credibility and illustration to the message of the gospel.

It is perfectly possible that the early church learned that the particular way it went about trying to show God's love to the poor had its dangers. Realisation of capital assets in the way they were doing may solve the problems of poverty in the short term, but it is not a very good long-term solution. Many commentators point out that fifteen years later we find Paul making a collection from the rich Christians in Greece for the poor Christians in Jerusalem. They speculate that after everybody had sold their land and given away their capital, there was not much to share but their poverty. It is not certain whether that is a fair analysis of the situation, but it is certainly true that we ought not to extrapolate the radical economic sharing described in the early chapters of Acts into a general rule of Christian conduct. This was an isolated early experiment; it is not the norm, even in the Book of Acts, and certainly not in the rest of the New Testament.

But though we need not copy this pattern of sharing in a direct way, we also have to beware lest criticism of the economic naïvety of this infant church makes us cynical about their actions. Here we find a group of men and women who have suddenly found an intoxicating love for one another which they express in extravagance, as lovers always do. It is quite pointless to tell the love-struck young romantic, when he is looking in the jeweller's window, 'You cannot afford it, you know. You will regret it,' for love sweeps all such computations aside. And if we have no experience of that kind of extravagant generosity, then while our economic arguments may be very sound, I doubt whether our hearts are. Maybe the finances of the church should challenge the prudence of the accountant more often than they do.

Of course love can be abused and certainly extravagance can be foolish. For the church to set itself up as an institution that encouraged begging was not wise. But even if the early church let its heart rule its head in this matter, at least it did have a heart. It set the gospel in the context of a deeply caring community.

St Ambrose, one of the early church fathers, rebuked the church of his day for the amount of money it spent on beautifying its church buildings, while neglecting the service of the poor. He said, 'A slave redeemed at the church's expense is a far better decoration for the Holy Communion table than a golden chalice!' Some of us may smugly congratulate ourselves that we do not go in for golden chalices, but then we do not go in much for redeeming slaves either.

Fellowship is not some mystical gas that pervades Christian meetings. It is the sense of belonging that comes from *doing* things with each other and from caring for each other. It's worth asking how much *fellowship* there is in our church. For we live in a world desperately longing for it.

3
Learning to Talk

Acts 3—4:31

*Then they called them in again and
commanded them not to speak or teach at
all in the name of Jesus. But Peter and
John replied, 'Judge for yourselves
whether it is right in God's sight to obey
you rather than God. For we cannot help
speaking about what we have seen and
heard.'*

Acts 4:18–20

FROM TIME to time we have all, I am sure, come across those evangelists who portray Jesus as the great problem solver. 'Come to Jesus, and all your worries will be over. You will get that promotion which you have been waiting for; you will pass those exams you have been studying for or you will find that Mr or Miss Right for whom you have been searching.' In short, whatever your wishes are, become a Christian and they will all come true, just as surely as if you had discovered Aladdin's magic lamp.

Of course, that is not the way it works as those of us who have been Christians for any length of time will know. There are many places in this world today where to become a Christian is likely to result in demotion, not promotion; where students are likely to find their educational career prematurely arrested rather than advanced; where the chance of finding a husband or wife, far from being improved, will be drastically reduced. There is a simple reason for this. Christianity talks. And the world, generally speaking, does not like religions that talk. It favours religion that is content to be hidden away in the secrecy of the individual's private life, and so pose no threat to the status quo.

Christianity, however, cannot be hidden away. The first thing the Holy Spirit did when he fell upon the apostles was to set their tongues wagging. Every opportunity they got, Peter and the others were standing up and speaking out in the name of Jesus. There is a typical example in Acts 3, where a cripple is healed by the apostles at the temple gate. A crowd of spectators quickly gathers to marvel at the event, and within a moment, Peter is on his feet, preaching the gospel just as he did on the Day of Pentecost. The response of his hearers is again prolific: 'Many who heard the message believed, and the number of men grew to about five thousand' (4:4).

This time, however, that positive response from the multitude is complemented by a new and more sinister audience:

> The priests and the captain of the temple guard and the Sadducees came up to Peter and John while they were speaking to the people. They were greatly disturbed because the apostles were teaching the people and proclaiming in Jesus the resurrection of the dead. They seized Peter and John...put them in jail (4:1–3).

The hostility commences

These verses are the signal that the honeymoon period of the early church is over. From now on, the infant church is going to find itself encountering increasingly violent opposition, culminating in the death of the first Christian martyr. The reasons for this gathering hostility from the Jewish authorities are various, and Luke alludes to several of them in the course of his narrative.

Intellectual snobbery seems to have played some part; notice that the apostles are referred to as 'unschooled, ordinary men' (4:13). That word 'unschooled' probably refers to the fact that they had no formal theological qualifications. And the word 'ordinary' in this context probably signifies that they had no official ecclesiastical office.

As far as the pompous academics in the Divinity Faculty at the University of Jerusalem were concerned, these apostles then were at best untrained laymen and, at worst, illiterate upstarts. Imagine how mortifying it must have been for them to observe that the apostles were attracting so much larger congregations to their open-air sermons than they could attract to their learned seminars: 'The high priest and all his associates...were filled with jealousy' (5:17).

Of course, the same holds good today. The academic establishment would be far less antagonistic towards Bible-believing Christianity if it were not so popular with those who are 'unschooled and ordinary'.

A second factor in the gathering opposition of the authorities was embarrassed indignation. The apostles would keep on reciting to their hearers the tale of how the Jewish establishment had conspired to get Jesus executed: 'You handed him over to be killed, and you disowned him before Pilate...You disowned the Holy and Righteous One and asked that a murderer be released to you. You killed the author of life' (3:13–14).

Not surprisingly, the Jewish council did not take kindly to these allegations, for not only did they threaten their political standing in the community, they were also uncomfortably close to the sordid truth. Luke spells out the defensiveness they were feeling: 'You...are determined to make us guilty of this man's blood' (5:28).

Even today, respectable people would be a good deal less offended by evangelical Christianity if it did not prick their consciences quite so effectively. The word 'sorry' always gets stuck in the collar of stuffed shirts.

Luke hints indirectly also at a third factor which may well have contributed to this gathering animosity. In 4:1 he specifically mentions that the Sadducees were prominent among the church's opponents, and in 5:17 he focuses even closer blame on this particular group, pointing out that the High Priest, and all his family, belonged to this party. This may well be significant, for one of the doctrinal distinctives of the Sadducees was that they did not believe in the resurrection of the dead. This was a major source of controversy between them and the other major Jewish party of those days, the Pharisees.

Imagine the consternation of those influential Sadducees when they found self-styled divinity lecturers Peter and John, not only teaching the people as if they were rabbis (for which they had no credentials whatsoever), but actually proclaiming the resurrection of the dead, not as a theory that was worth considering, but as an established truth of divine revelation which Jewish orthodoxy should no longer doubt. Even today, there are many people who would be far less hostile to Christianity if it did not challenge their preconceived ideas so dogmatically. If only Christians would say 'perhaps' and 'in my opinion' rather more often and tone down that strident 'thus saith the Lord' note in their preaching. How can a sceptic sustain his self-respect in the face of such uncompromising certainty?

All these factors, then, play a part in the gathering storm, but the principal reason the Jewish authorities tried to silence the apostles is that given in 4:17: 'To stop this thing from spreading any further among the people, we must warn these men to speak no longer to anyone in this name.'

That was what really bothered them: Christianity was a religion that talked and, because it talked, it was growing. Already, its circles of influence were beginning to expand at an alarming rate. And it is important that we realise there are spiritual forces in our world which have a vested interest in halting those ever-increasing circles. The New Testament makes it clear that since the birth of Jesus this world has become the arena of a cosmic battle. As Paul says in his letter to the Ephesians, 'our struggle is not against flesh and blood, but against the rulers, against the authorities, against the powers of this dark world and against the spiritual forces of evil in the heavenly realms' (Eph 6:12). Behind the malice of the Jews here, there is no question but that Luke sees the malice of demonic forces that want the kingdom of God restricted and suffocated. And that means shutting up the Christians. Christianity grows because it talks; stop it talking and you stop it growing.

But the remarkable thing is, they couldn't stop it talking. As hard as they tried to intimidate this young church into silence, they simply could not do it: 'For we cannot help speaking about what we have seen and heard' (4:20).

What was it that gave them the courage to go on witnessing to Christ in spite of the very real threat of persecution and even death? Luke in these chapters gives us five insights on the point.

The incontrovertible evidence of a changed life

> 'Rulers and elders of the people! If we are being called to account today for an act of kindness shown to a cripple and are asked how he was healed, then know this, you and everyone else in Israel: It is by the name of Jesus Christ of Nazareth, whom you crucified but whom God raised from the dead, that this man stands before you completely healed' (4:8–10).

This is a reference to that healing of the cripple which is recorded in chapter 3 and which had happened the day before. The cripple was a congenitally handicapped man who, we are told, was placed daily at the gate of the temple, begging for alms from those who went in to worship. Luke comments that it was the gate called 'Beautiful' which he patronised, intending perhaps a rather subtle irony; for though this portico may have been pretty, it was pretty useless as far as the cripple was concerned. For all its ornate decoration, it had no answer to his helpless condition. Luke may even have seen in it an illustration of the spectacular religion of rules and rituals to which it gave entrance; a religion that was also spectacularly powerless to change a human life.

When Peter and John came to the gate, however, they turned this cripple's world upside-down: 'Silver or gold I do not have, but what I have I give you. In the name of Jesus Christ of Nazareth, walk' (3:6).

For the first time in forty years, this man passed through that gate he knew so well, into the temple courts beyond. So delirious with joy at his new-found mobility was he, he went leaping and praising God. Peter is quick to seize the opportunity and speaks to the rapidly-gathering crowds: 'Men of Israel, why does this surprise you? Why do you stare at us as if by our own power or godliness we had made this man walk?...It is Jesus' name and the faith that comes through him that has given this complete healing to him, as you can all see' (3:12,16).

There is no more cogent apologetic for the Christian faith than a testimony like that to a changed life; not then, in first-century Jerusalem, or now, in twentieth-century England. I am not suggesting of course that the only way to convince people of the truth of Christianity is to work a miracle of healing before every sermon. Though there are some in the so-called 'Signs and Wonders' movement who would be rather sympathetic to that point of view, I believe they have grossly overstated their case. Even in New Testament times, miracles of this sort were comparatively rare, and they were very closely associated, as we have already said, with the unique role of the apostles as divinely accredited spokesmen of God. I do not dispute that supernatural events can and do still occur, but the fact is that nobody is healing congenital cripples today in the way that this man was healed, and we would be cruelly deluding many thousands of handicapped people if we were to pretend otherwise.

Nevertheless, notwithstanding the fact that in the twentieth century we are not in the apostolic age, and we are unlikely therefore to witness miracles of the same calibre as the apostles were able to perform for that reason, the general truth which this story illustrates is still valid. Jesus changes lives. He changes them dramatically, and people notice.

There is a very good illustration of that in Keith Miller's book *The Habitation of Dragons*. He tells us how he was used in the conversion of a business man called Joe in the USA. About a year after his conversion, Joe wrote to Miller saying that Jesus had really changed him, and he was trying to put his life in order according to the Bible. He had started to share his faith with some business colleagues, but being inexperienced as a Christian, and inarticulate, he could not get across satisfactorily what it was all about. So he asked Miller if he would return to his town and speak at an informal meeting to which he could invite some of his friends and acquaintances from the commercial world to whom he had been trying to witness.

Miller tells us he was not very keen on the idea because he had a very heavy schedule on the other side of the country at that time and it would be a long journey to undertake for the sake of addressing a private lunch party, but somewhat reluctantly he did agree to go. When the day arrived, the plane was late, and he had to be hustled from the airport straight onto the platform. He tells us that as he strode to the lectern, he was stunned by the sight that greeted him. He had come to a private luncheon party for a few of Joe's friends. But there before him were 800 men gathered in the hotel lounge. They were all colleagues of Joe, people with whom he had been trying to share his faith. Miller writes, 'At that moment I realised that all the evangelistic promotions, programmes and campaigns in the world are virtually worthless to motivate people to become Christians unless they see some ordinary person like Joe who is finding a new way to live in Christ.'

People do not come to listen to preachers because

their oratory is powerful, or their arguments are clever. They come because they have seen lives transformed by Jesus, and are curious to find out about it. And as Peter demonstrates very clearly in our reading here, any preacher who can point to such a transformed life is in an unassailable position when it comes to facing the opposition: 'Since they could see the man who had been healed standing there with them, there was nothing they could say' (4:14). ' "What are we going to do with these men?" they asked. "Everybody living in Jerusalem knows they have done an outstanding miracle, and we cannot deny it" ' (4:16).

Faced with such indisputable support, their objections to these Christian preachers are exposed as mere donnish bigotry. Whether they are prepared to admit it or not, the name of Jesus had changed the man radically, permanently and supernaturally. There is no answer to the incontrovertible evidence of a changed life.

The incomparable authority of the risen Jesus

> Know this, you and everyone else in Israel: It is by the name of Jesus Christ of Nazareth, whom you crucified but whom God raised from the dead, that this man stands before you completely healed (4:10).

I want you to notice how Peter moves from talking about the cripple to talking about Christ. Compelling though the evidence of the healed cripple is, it is not enough. Both in his sermons to the crowd, and in his defence to the Jewish Sanhedrin, Peter uses the evidence of the cripple only as a pointer to direct his audience to some even more important pieces of evidence, namely the death and the resurrection of Jesus Christ: 'He is the stone you builders rejected, which has become the capstone. Salvation is found in no-one else, for there is no other name under heaven given to men by which we must be saved' (4:11–12).

This is a vital observation for though testimony is a powerful introduction to evangelism, it is not evangelism. Testimony is telling people what Jesus has done for me in my personal experience, but evangelism is telling people what Jesus has done for the world in history. Many Christians are led into confusion about this as a result of the loose use of that word 'witness'. When the apostles talked about being witnesses, they meant it in a sense quite different from the way in which we may use that word today. When they spoke of themselves as witnesses, it invariably referred to their first-hand knowledge of the foundational events of the Christian faith, the things they had 'seen and heard' (4:20). 'You disowned the Holy and Righteous One and asked that a murderer be released to you. You killed the author of life, but God raised him from the dead. We are *witnesses* of this' (3:14–15, italics mine).

Clearly Christians today cannot be witnesses of that first Good Friday and that first Easter Sunday in such an objective sense. Our experience of Jesus is real, but we are not eye-witnesses like those who stood by the empty tomb. So when we speak of witness, we mean something different from what the apostles meant by it. Ours is the same kind of testimony which the healed cripple provided; a testimony to our personal experience of what Jesus has done in our lives. But if we are going to be New Testament evangelists, we must go beyond that to affirm, as Peter does here, what Jesus has done for the world in his saving work. By raising him from the dead, God has marked Jesus out as uniquely and exclusively the Lord and Saviour of all mankind: 'Salvation is found in no-one else, for there is no other name under heaven given to men by which we must be saved' (4:12).

That is the gospel; not the special experience that *I* have received from him, but the eternal salvation which he provides for anybody and everybody who calls on his name.

There is a great danger in these days when New Age ideas are becoming so rampant, that the gospel will be presented by careless Christians as just another variety of religious experience. I remember many years ago, when I was a travelling secretary with the University and Colleges Christian Unions, that I visited a student group which was trying to deal with one of the Eastern sects which sprang up on many campuses in the seventies. Some of the CU members there were trying very hard to witness to fellow students who had been caught up in this particular variety of oriental mysticism, but their efforts, though well intentioned, were failing. This is how their conversations tended to go: 'Oh, you should come along and hear my guru,' said the mystic devotee. 'He gives you a real mind-blowing spiritual experience; I know—I have had it.'

'No, no,' replied the Christian, 'your guru is a fake. You should come along to our CU meeting. Jesus gives you a real spiritual experience.'

You see, they were just swapping testimonies, setting one experience against another. What they failed to realise is that what that Hindu group lacked was not spiritual experience, but history. There was no cross or resurrection in their message. All they had was purple bubbles of mystical ecstasy inside their meditating eyeballs. And the Christians were foolishly talking as if all Jesus could offer was better bubbles!

It is because of the unique historical events of that first Easter weekend that Peter can say so confidently, 'There is no salvation in anybody else. There is no other name under heaven given to men by which we must be saved.' Do you notice that word 'must'? Peter is not talking about some optional spiritual experience, but about a radical moral rescue which we must have, or perish under the judgement of God. Because of the supreme authority he wields— because of the unique place in the universe he occupies—we neglect Jesus at our peril.

Peter and the other apostles were so hard to shut up because they knew this. To have yielded to the authorities' intimidation and stopped preaching about this Jesus would have been the height of irresponsibility. There was a 'must' about him. He was the most important thing that had ever happened in the history of the world.

I know the phrase 'Jesus saves' has a quaint, almost Victorian, sound at the end of the twentieth century. But I assure you those words are of such importance that over the centuries thousands of Christian preachers have been prepared to suffer and die so that they might be heard. The risen Jesus possesses an incomparable authority, and they just *had* to talk about it.

> They called them in again and commanded them not
> to speak or teach at all in the name of Jesus. But Peter
> and John replied, 'Judge for yourselves whether it is
> right in God's sight to obey you rather than God. For
> we cannot help speaking about what we have seen and
> heard' (4:18–20).

This response of the apostles to the authorities'
demand that they stop preaching is extremely significant. It has repercussions for our whole understanding of the nature and limits of civil authority. It
has always been a problem for political scientists to
determine how far the individual ought to go in
obeying the state. The issue was raised some years
ago with the debate on the war crimes bill in the
House of Commons. During the Nuremburg Trials,
when many war criminals from Nazi Germany were
tried, some of those officers pleaded 'not guilty' on
the grounds that they were ordered to do what they
did, and therefore could not be held responsible for
what happened.

By pleading that way, they were appealing to a
view of the state which is very ancient and which
finds one of its most extreme expressions in fascism.
This view says that the state has a life and will of its
own with which every citizen must co-operate or
perish; the individual exists to serve the state. Some
of its advocates even come close to deifying the state,
regarding it as 'the march of God in the world'
(Hegel). And such a philosophy played no small part
in the development of Hitler's Germany.

What Peter and John are saying here, however,
implies that Christians must reject that view of the

state. We cannot treat the state as an absolute authority which the citizen must obey. Rather, as Christian citizens, we reserve the right to disobey the civil authority when it exceeds its legitimate God-given role.

This I say is a very significant step, and one which has made an enormous contribution to our contemporary ideas of liberty. Notice carefully the grounds the apostles cite for their defiance. First they appeal to *freedom of conscience*. 'Judge for yourselves whether it is right' (4:19) they ask, the implication being, 'And we shall judge for ourselves too.' No one should do anything which in their heart of hearts they know is wrong. Peter and John would not stop preaching the gospel for the same reason the accused Nazi officers should have refused to put prisoners in the gas chamber: for conscience sake. Men and women are responsible agents; they must judge for themselves what is right and cannot allow themselves to become puppets, manipulated by others.

Secondly, there is an appeal to *freedom of religion*. 'Judge for yourselves whether it is right in God's sight to obey you rather than God' (4:19). Peter and John's convictions were religious in nature, rooted in their convictions about God, and it is of the very nature of religious commitment that it demands uncompromising allegiance. If a person believes that God requires such and such a thing, he cannot refuse, even if the state prohibits it, for to do so would be to turn the state into an idol, placing it above God in his scale of priorities.

Thirdly, there is an appeal to *freedom of speech*. 'For we cannot help speaking about what we have seen and heard' (4:20). A man or woman who knows certain things are true must bear testimony to what he or she knows, or sacrifice his or her self-respect and human integrity. 'Silence these,' said Jesus of his disciples, 'and the very stones would cry out.' The truth is more important than the convenience of civil authorities; censorship of the gospel is similarly unacceptable.

The Christian citizen, because of his worldview, must reserve the right of civil disobedience against the situation in which the state exceeds its God-given role.

Notice, however, that Peter and John do not quarrel here with the right of the state to imprison them. They do not appeal to freedom of conscience, or of religion, or of speech as if these were constitutional rights that no government could refuse. The Bible nowhere insists that the state must be a pluralistic institution practising our modern idea of toleration. If a state is ideologically committed to a religion or philosophy other than Christianity, as this Jewish state was, then it is extremely likely that they will put Christians in prison, either for heresy or treason.

In fact, confronted by the church, the state has only three alternatives: persecution, conversion or toleration. None, I think, is really satisfactory to the Christian; not even conversion, as the Constantinian period proves. The church is not a secular institution and so perhaps will always be an anomaly in this age; an angular feature in any political environment. The one thing no state can ever succeed in doing, however, is to silence the Christians. For though they are loyal to their nation and respectful to their governments, they are citizens of heaven first, and obey God rather than men.

Regrettably, on those occasions down through history when the Christian church itself has wielded political power, it has not always allowed the free-doms Peter and John are claiming for themselves here. In dealing with heretics and infidels, it has sometimes itself been the perpetrator of persecution. But notwithstanding that failure of the institutional church to accept the consequences of Peter's words here, it is also true that there have been many humble Christians down through history who have understood the stand the apostles took here and have emulated it. The civil liberties which we take for granted in this country have been bought largely at the price of their suffering. Christians are not anarch-ists who despise the state, but free citizens who refuse to offer the state blind obedience. Consider for example the famous words of Andrew Melville with which he rebuked King James VI of Scotland for his attempted interference in the affairs of the church in the seventeenth century:

> We must discharge our duty, or else be traitors both to Christ and you, for there are two kings in Scotland. There is King James, the head of the Commonwealth, and there is Christ Jesus, the King of the church, whose subject James VI is, of whose kingdom he is not a lord, not a king, but a member. We will yield to you your place, and give you all due obedience, but you are not the head of the church, you cannot give eternal life, nor can you deprive us of it. We charge you, therefore, to permit us freely to meet and to preach in Christ's name.

That is the kind of aggressive defiance of which a Christian is capable, because he understands what it means to be a free man under God; honouring the king, but not licking his boots.

'Sovereign Lord,' they said, 'you made the heaven and
the earth and the sea, and everything in them. You
spoke by the Holy Spirit through the mouth of your
servant, our father David:
  "Why do the nations rage and
     the peoples plot in vain?
  The kings of the earth take their stand
  and the rulers gather together
     against the Lord
     and against his Anointed One" ' (4:24–26).

David wrote those words from Psalm 2 a thousand
years before in days when hostile nations threatened
the young kingdom of Israel. 'Such opposition,'
wrote David, 'is impudent. How dare these foreign
powers arraign themselves against the Lord Jehovah
and his chosen King?' More than that, it is futile.
How can they possibly hope to succeed? For the
people plot in vain when they take their stand
'against the Lord and his Anointed One'.

As the young church experiences persecution for
the first time, it seizes on exactly the same sentiment
and applies it to its own situation. Indeed, it seems to
see David's words as prophetic. The Christians see
themselves as God's true people, and Jesus as God's
true Son, the anointed Messiah. Herod and Pilate
now represent those alien powers conspiring against
the people of God; against the Lord and his Anointed
One. Just as that conspiracy was doomed in David's
day, so it is now, for in spite of all their machina-
tions, God cannot be thwarted. How can you outwit
omniscience or defeat omnipotence? It is impossible;
they 'plot in vain'.

These early Christians of course had the very

obvious example of the cross in their own recent experience to show just how foolish was the attempt to thwart God's purpose: 'Herod and Pontius Pilate met together with the Gentiles and the people of Israel in this city to conspire against your holy servant Jesus, whom you anointed. They did what your power and will had decided beforehand should happen' (4:27–28).

They thought they had won when they put Jesus on the cross, but God was not taken by surprise. God took the malice of the Jews, and the impotence of Pilate, and wove them into his great plan of redemption. He was, you see, what they began by calling him, 'the Sovereign Lord'.

In the original Greek, the word for 'sovereign' is *despot*. A rather unexpected term with many unpleasant connotations. But Christians do believe in dictatorship: the dictatorship of God. He alone has absolute power and constrains obedience by virtue of his irresistible strength and his unimpeachable justice. He controls the wheels of history; of that these early Christians were absolutely certain. And there is no recipe for courage like faith in such a God.

If he could turn the cross from a defeat into a victory, then there is no set-back that can possibly hinder the advance of his purposes in the world. Let them put the whole church in prison if they want to, they will only achieve what God decided beforehand should happen.

People who really believe in a sovereign God like that are fearless and intimidated by nobody. No matter how big his army, or how lofty his throne, they cannot be frightened. Chrysostom, the early church father, was on trial for his life. The Emperor said, 'We will banish you!'

And Chrysostom is reputed to have replied, 'You cannot banish me for the whole world is my Father's home.'

'Well then, we will execute you,' said the Emperor.

'You cannot,' he replied. 'My life is hid with Christ.'

'Well then, we will dispossess you of your estate.'

'You cannot,' he said. 'I have not got any. All my treasure is in heaven.'

'Well then, we will put you in solitary confinement,' said the Emperor.

'You cannot, for I have a divine Friend from whom you can never separate me. I defy you, there is nothing you can do to hurt me.'

Such is the defiance of Christians who know what a sovereign God they have.

It will be a great day for Christendom in this land when once again we Christians demonstrate that kind of courage. Perhaps we do not have it because the opposition seems more remote somehow. Now we have religious toleration we can hide very successfully and nobody bothers about us. We can get by in this world without facing any opposition at all if we want to. If we just keep quiet nothing will ever be done to hurt us and no one will ever raise a word against us. It is only talkative Christians who encounter opposition, but the closer we live to the leading edge of missionary endeavour and church growth, the hotter that opposition will become. If it is our ambition to make a real contribution to the growth of the kingdom of God in this world in our generation, then like Peter we will face hostility. Better be ready for it.

A dynamic experience of the Holy Spirit

> Peter, filled with the Holy Spirit, said...(4:8).

> They were all filled with the Holy Spirit and spoke the word of God boldly (4:31).

You must have seen those adverts that exploit the 'before' and 'after' picture. Before, the girl, potentially attractive, is sitting at the dance feeling jaded and rejected. Then she discovers the secret factor she needs: 'Glamour Girl hair-spray'. One whiff and the whole scene is transformed. She oozes self-confidence and is surrounded by admirers. Or, 'before', the man is being deluged with bills, showing anxiety all over his stress-ridden face. Then he discovers the secret of success: 'The Clapham & Wandsworth Building Society'. A quick investment of the odd fiver or two, and his economic difficulties dissolve over night. Once again he can look his family in the face and smile at the world. It is all nonsense of course, as adverts frequently are, but it does show how many people privately feel unhappy with themselves, are unfulfilled or are lacking confidence and wish they were different. The advertisers are trying to exploit that psychological feature by assuring us that all we need is hair spray, or a building society, but we know that is not true.

Is there anything, then, that can really change us, shake us out of the apathy and the timidity of our natural personalities, and inject enthusiasm and confidence into us? Without such a transformation it is quite clear there is no way the ripples of Jesus are going to reach the ends of the earth.

Just consider the disciples the day before Pentecost. They were demoralised and defeated; in spite of Jesus' resurrection, they were not fundamentally different people. Then Pentecost came, and quite suddenly we find them out on the streets shouting their heads off, even being mistaken for drunkards. Think particularly of Peter. Who would have thought this was the man who only a few weeks before had been denying he even knew Jesus, so intimidated had he been by the accusation of a serving girl. Yet now we find him lifting up his voice so everybody can hear. What has happened to turn this coward skulking in the Upper Room into a courageous preacher?

The Spirit had come! Again and again in these early chapters of Acts we find the phrase 'filled with the Spirit' and on every occasion it is used in the context of Christians finding supernatural resources of confidence to proclaim Christ in the public arena.

It is important to realise that the early church did not have a missionary arm for it was a missionary movement. The whole show was very amateur— they did not employ professional experts—but the Spirit made them into effective communicators. He injected into them the courage, enthusiasm and eloquence they needed.

Such filling of the Holy Spirit is going to be vital in our generation too if the task of world evangelism is to be completed. For our job is as difficult as was that of the apostles. As a result of the missionary movement of the last 200 years, generally speaking the easy places in the world have now been reached. The remaining masses of the unreached now lie embedded in very hostile places, often riddled with demonic power and superstition; countries which cannot be entered with the label 'missionary' on the passport any longer. In many areas which have yet to be reached, it is impossible to preach the gospel publicly without committing an act of civil disobedience as the apostles had to. In many of them, to be known as a Christian is to risk imprisonment or even death. If such places are to be penetrated it will require people who, like Peter, are burning with a huge enthusiasm and fired by a great courage. Where will we find those men and women if it is not through the Holy Spirit coming afresh on individuals and making them different?

The power of the Holy Spirit, however, is also vital for those of us whom God calls to more modest lives of witness in our own families and neighbourhoods. Some years ago, John Stott wrote a little booklet in which he outlined very well the frustration that many feel in personal witness. We want to share our faith, and we know we ought to share our faith, but our tongues are tied, as he put it, by *Our Guilty Silence*. What is it that inhibits us? Is it our natural shyness, our apathy, our fear of other people or our inferiority complex? All of these things were characteristic of the early disciples too, but the Spirit transformed them into people who *talked* about their faith.

And it is clear from what Peter says at the end of his Pentecost sermon that there is no reason why we should not know more of that same power of the Spirit to make us witnesses too.

When the people heard this, they were cut to the heart and said to Peter and the other apostles, 'Brothers, what shall we do?' Peter replied, 'Repent and be baptised, every one of you, in the name of Jesus Christ so that your sins may be forgiven. And you will receive the gift of the Holy Spirit. The promise is for you and your children and for all who are far off—for all whom the Lord our God will call' (2:37–39).

The Holy Spirit did not limit himself to the apostles. He is still available.

A little boy once asked a sailor, 'What is the wind?'

'I don't really understand it,' the sailor replied. 'But I can hoist a sail.'

Perhaps that is what we need to do. We cannot fathom the mystery of the Holy Spirit, but we like Peter can experience the dynamic power for witness which he represents.

4

Nobody's Perfect

Acts 5—6:7

More and more men and women believed in the Lord and were added to their number.

Acts 5:14

There are two recipes for success in church growth that are popular today, and they are both wrong.

One recipe says that success can be achieved simply by virtue of good organisation. Churches that believe this have vast programmes of activities requiring dozens of memos, schedules and committees. The minister of such a church has a lot in common with a company director. Indeed, it's not impossible that he was in the boardroom before he became a pastor. And if he wasn't, he has certainly been on a course in business administration since. He spends most of his week making sure the wheels of the organisation keep turning smoothly, like a kind of human oil-can. He doesn't get much time to read, or study, or pray for that matter. And his family doesn't see him much either. But then organisation men have that problem in every walk of life.

Churches like this often achieve an illusion of success; everything seems bright and dynamic. But when you dig beneath the surface a little, frequently you discover something missing—the something that makes a machine different from a body, namely *life*! A church isn't just an organisation, it's an organism. Its unity derives from a shared Spirit, not just a common timetable.

If, however, success cannot be achieved by good organisation, there are other churches that make the very opposite mistake. They say that success can be achieved without any organisation at all. Such churches make much of spontaneity. They don't have official leaders—everyone just does 'as they feel led'. There is no planning of the budget, for 'the Lord will provide'. No one prepares a sermon—it is more spiritual to rely on immediate inspiration, and Bible study smacks far too much of legalism. Better by far to have unstructured times of 'sharing'. All in all, the rule is 'do your own thing' and don't worry too much about what others are doing.

There is no doubt it can be rather exciting to belong to a group like this, especially for individuals who are frustrated by the tedium and monotony of an over-regulated lifestyle. But once again the success is only surface deep. For while there may very well be life in such groups, it is undirected life. The random activity of a victim of St Vitus' dance. A body is not a machine, it's true, but there is order and control. It cannot be just a random collection of limbs each 'doing their own thing'. There has to be a central nervous system and a directing intelligence, or all you have is unco-ordinated spasticity.

Organisation and discipline then are no substitute for life, but they are an indispensable condition for effective living. The same is true in the body of Christ. We model the church neither on the computerised precision of a robot, nor on the haphazard antics of a mentally deranged chimpanzee. A healthy church is an organised organism. And you could not ask for a better model of a congregation working that out in practice than the infant church in the early chapters of the Book of Acts.

In the last chapter we observed the spontaneous life which the Holy Spirit breathed into this new community. Nowhere was it more obvious than in the generous way they voluntarily met the material needs of the poor among them. But ironically it was that very welfare programme which eventually high-lighted the importance of organisation and discipline among them.

Quality control

> Now a man named Ananias, together with his wife Sapphira, also sold a piece of property. With his wife's full knowledge he kept back part of the money for himself, but brought the rest and put it at the apostles' feet (Acts 5:1–2).

In a group that was growing as rapidly as the early church it was inevitable that a few rotten apples should get into the pile. How a community disci-plines such corrupt members is vital to its long-term future. Is there going to be accountability and the enforcement of certain standards? If not, the move-ment, whatever its early idealism, will degenerate into something which is no different from the rest of the world.

For the early church it was the incident of Ananias and Sapphira which brought this issue of discipline to a head.

It is important to understand the reason for the conspiracy between this couple. Clearly it was not simple greed, because as Peter points out they were under no obligation to sell their field, nor were they required to devote all the proceeds of the sale to the church: 'Didn't it belong to you before it was sold? And after it was sold, wasn't the money at your disposal?' (5:4).

If we were in any doubt about the essentially voluntarist nature of the early church's communalism that verse settles the matter.

It seems possible then that the action of Ananias and Sapphira was prompted not by avarice but jealousy. At the end of chapter 4 Luke records that Barnabas, an eminent member of the early church, had just sold a field and laid the money at the apostles' feet. No doubt Barnabas got a lot of congratulation for doing that, and reading a little between the lines, it is possible that Ananias and Sapphira were found grinding their teeth with envy as a result. They wanted the reputation of being philanthropists too, and that is why they hatched this pathetic little plot. The sale of their property was motivated not by any genuine sensitivity to the needs of others, but rather by an exhibitionist desire to parade their virtue like the hypocrite who blew his trumpet to announce that he was giving a gift in the temple treasury.

Jealousy alone, however, is not enough to explain what happened either. For Ananias and Sapphira went beyond merely having the wrong motive for what they were doing; they wanted to have their cake and to eat it too. Much as they wished to be ranked with Barnabas in the esteem of the Christian community, they bridled at the monetary sacrifice involved and so devised their deception, confident it seems that they could fool the church and the apostles, and even pull the wool over God's eyes! But they were terribly wrong.

Then Peter said, 'Ananias, how is it that Satan has so filled your heart that you have lied to the Holy Spirit and have kept for yourself some of the money you received for the land?...What made you think of doing such a thing? You have not lied to men, but to God.' When Ananias heard this, he fell down and died (5:3–5).

In order that we may be clear this was a divine judgement and not just a coincidental heart attack, Luke goes on to record how precisely the same fate befell his wife:

About three hours later his wife came in, not knowing what had happened. Peter asked her, 'Tell me, is this the price you and Ananias got for the land?'

'Yes,' she said, 'that is the price.'

Peter said to her, 'How could you agree to test the Spirit of the Lord? Look! The feet of the men who buried your husband are at the door, and they will carry you out also.'

At that moment she fell down at his feet and died. Then the young men came in and, finding her dead, carried her out and buried her beside her husband (5:7–10).

The savageness of this stroke of judgement shocks many Christians. Indeed, it undoubtedly had the same effect on the early church because we read: 'And great fear seized all who heard what had happened' (5:5). 'Great fear seized the whole church and all who heard about these events' (5:11).

It is not impossible that Luke has in mind a similar incident which is recorded in the Book of Joshua. There we read of Achan who stole some treasure from Jericho which was supposed to be dedicated to

God. As a result the Israelite community suffered continual defeat in battle, until at last his greed and deception were discovered, and he and his family were executed for his crime. People have difficulty with that story too, but in many ways it parallels this incident. Luke may very well be deliberately alluding to it, for the word he uses here for 'keeping back' (v 3) is the very word which the Book of Joshua uses for what Achan did in 'keeping back' those trinkets from Jericho.

The point is that the people of God are a disciplined company. To fulfil the purpose which God has for them they must maintain a much higher standard of conduct than is tolerated in the world. That is why in the Old Testament Israel was commanded to invoke the death penalty for some crimes which, in our so-called 'enlightened age', we would regard as minor offences. The reason often given for the severity of such punishments is interesting: 'Purge the evil from among you. All Israel will hear of it and be afraid' (Deut 21:21). Those severe punishments were imposed on certain kinds of wrong behaviour in order to purify the people and to deter others who might be tempted. God's people had to be different: their moral superiority had to be maintained.

In the New Testament days, of course, the church has no recourse to the power of the sword. But that is not to be interpreted as implying that in Christ liberalised standards of conduct are sanctioned within the community of God's people. God is just as strict and expects the same kind of discipline among his New Testament people as he did long ago among the Jews. Just as that greedy Israelite was stoned to death for hoarding Canaanite trinkets, so Ananias and Sapphira died. Thereby an obelisk of warning is erected at the very beginning of the church's life indicating to all that this is a sanctified company. The church of God, founded on the twelve apostles, is holy, just as the Israel founded on the twelve patriarchs was holy. Rotten apples must be purged from the pile so that 'all...will hear of it and be afraid'.

Not all local congregations today take this matter with anything like the seriousness the story of Ananias and Sapphira demands. God will not have the purity of his church adulterated by hypocrites. He expects the church to be made up of the genuine article. Sometimes, of course, anxiety-prone Christians accuse themselves of hypocrisy unnecessarily. They are very sensitive about sin in their lives, and as a result every time they enter church on a Sunday they say to themselves, 'I should not be here. I have got no right to be here. I am a hypocrite.' That is not, of course, the case. They would only be guilty of hypocrisy if they were deliberately pretending to be something they were not. There is no expectation on the part of any Christian congregation that everybody who walks through the doors will be perfect. The church is a hospital for sinners, not a shop window for ready-made angels. There are many things in all of our lives that make us feel ashamed. But that does not make us hypocrites whom God is going to strike dead. It was the element of *deceit* that made the crime of this couple so heinous.

The one thing the church does have the right to expect of every member is honesty. God will not have his church cluttered up with people pretending to be what they are not. The world is not offended to discover that Christians have faults, but it is mightily offended to find Christians with faults parading themselves as Holy Joes who have none. It is those who seek to cloak their sin under a mask of moral respectability that the church must discipline. Sin that is frankly confessed and repented of must always be forgiven. But never try to lie to the Holy Spirit, for even if the church cannot discover your secret shame and discipline you for it, God will.

Grievance procedure

> In those days when the number of disciples was increasing, the Grecian Jews among them complained against those of the Aramaic-speaking community because their widows were being overlooked in the daily distribution of food (6:1).

Close on the heels of the first case of church discipline comes the first need for a church business meeting. And once again it is the welfare programme that is the source of the trouble. There were two communities of Jews in the early church. The distinction between them went back two or three hundred years to the time when Jews had been forced to decide how they should respond to the challenge of the Greek culture which had been introduced as a result of the conquests of Alexander the Great. Some had taken a very conservative line, insisting that they should retain Aramaic as their primary language and refuse to absorb the manners of the Greek empire. Others, however, more pragmatically, were prepared to speak Greek and engage in international commerce. Many Jews were by this time scattered around Asia and Europe anyway, and had little choice but to accommodate to the prevailing secular culture. These two groups of Jews were often at loggerheads with one another. The Aramaic-speaking community based in Jerusalem tended to have a superior attitude, feeling that they were less contaminated by paganism than their Hellenistic cousins. And the inferiority complex which some Greek-speaking Jews felt as a result seems to have spilled over into church politics. The apostles, you see, all belonged to the Aramaic group, at least by background, having been raised in Palestine. The Greek-speaking contingent were quick to attribute any inequity to sectarian partiality. 'We're not getting a fair deal in the welfare programme,' they insisted. 'The Palestinian widows are getting more food than ours are! You're treating us as second-class citizens—it's discrimination, that's what it is!'

It is doubtful in the extreme that there was any deliberate policy of discrimination being practised by the apostles. What is much more likely is that they were grossly over-extended in managing this rapidly multiplying congregation. After all, there were now well over 5,000 church members (4:4) and the numbers were growing all the time. The twelve apostles were still the only official leaders of the movement, so this vast company looked to them to do everything, from preaching the sermons to running the church finances. It is not surprising that we find evidences of strain as a result.

The situation was clearly already frustrating the apostles themselves, for they simply could not find time to give the attention they should to the spiritual aspects of their task. Hence we find them commenting: 'It would not be right for us to neglect the ministry of the word of God in order to wait on tables' (6:2).

This is not a haughty 'such things are beneath important people like us' kind of remark. The apostles were perfectly prepared to undertake menial tasks if they had time. But as apostles they did have a unique role which demanded that they put first things first. As the God-appointed teachers of the church they could not afford to neglect the ministry of the word, but the pressures of the welfare programme were in danger of eroding that vital priority. As is so often the case, busy people were finding that urgent things easily usurp important things.

But it was the effects of the apostles' over-work on the congregation as a whole which were most potentially dangerous. Luke hints at just how explosive the resentment which the Greek speaking groups were feeling could have become by once again making a subtle allusion to the time of the Exodus. He uses the same word for 'complained (v 1) as is used in the Books of Exodus and Numbers of the 'murmuring' of the children of Israel in the wilderness. Those complaints, as every Jew knew, led eventually to a whole generation being condemned to die in the desert outside the Promised Land. Would it be the same story all over again? Fortunately not, for just as Moses learned the art of delegation (Ex 18:24–26), so the apostles brought in additional personnel to assist them in the leadership of God's people.

Up until now the church had possessed a very informal administrative structure. They shared a spontaneous community life together which was without doubt vibrant and exciting. But when interpersonal problems of one sort and another begin to arise, it is necessary for authority structures, job descriptions and grievance procedures to be in place. You have to have leaders allocated whose responsibility it is to sort such problems out, or the unity of the group can be seriously undermined. So we find here the early church for the first time discovering its need of organisation. The apostles summon the first church meeting: 'The Twelve gathered all the disciples together...' (6:2). And put a proposal to the assembly: 'Brothers, choose seven men from among you who are known to be full of the Spirit and wisdom. We will turn this responsibility over to them...' (6:3).

It demonstrated considerable humility on the part of the apostles that they were prepared to act in this way. Delegation is not the strong point of every leader. It would not have been unnatural had Peter and the others adopted an injured, 'Oh, so you don't think we are doing our jobs properly, eh?' sort of tone. Some leaders get themselves enmeshed in a kind of indispensability syndrome which makes them insist they must do everything. Sometimes it is selfish ambition that generates it; more often it is a perfectionist over-conscientiousness that fears others are bound to get it wrong. But either way it takes real humility to surrender control, and these apostles had that quality.

Notice too the calibre of the seven men they chose. They had to be 'full of the Spirit and wisdom'. Looking after the church's poor relief fund may seem like a fairly minor task, but in the church it demanded the best people they had. What is even more startling though is that, judging by the names given in verse 5, all seven were representatives of the Greek-speaking community who were feeling aggrieved: 'They chose Stephen, a man full of faith and of the Holy Spirit; also Philip, Procorus, Nicanor, Timon, Parmenas, and Nicholas from Antioch, a convert to Judaism' (6:5).

Not only are these all Greek names, one of them

we are distinctly told was not even a Jew by birth. Nicholas of Antioch was a Gentile proselyte. What a tribute to the Aramaic-speaking community that they could agree so unanimously to such an irenical gesture. It would be a bit like a white church in South Africa appointing a black treasurer.

Notice it was not the apostles themselves who suggested these seven names. The initiative in the matter came from the congregation. 'They chose...' (v 5), though the apostles' authority was acknowledged in the appointment: 'They presented these men to the apostles, who prayed and laid their hands on them' (6:6).

And note the profound effect which Luke implies this decision had on the church's wider ministry: 'So the word of God spread. The number of disciples in Jerusalem increased rapidly, and a large number of priests became obedient to the faith' (6:7).

The implication of that word 'So...' at the beginning of verse 7 seems to be that there was some causal connection between the expanding circles of the church's evangelistic effectiveness in the city, and this organisational step they had taken. No, social action is not evangelism. And organisation cannot in and of itself make churches grow. But the way the church responds to social needs, and the way it handles internal problems, and the way it cares for vulnerable groups within its membership— such things are observed by outsiders and either enhance the credibility of the preached message or contradict it. A congregation that goes out of its way to ensure that concern is expressed practically, impartially and efficiently to those in material need is a church which by its organisation proves itself to be truly alive. And a church like that is going to grow.

Grass-roots enthusiasm is vital; but discipline and order are necessary too to channel it in ways that are not self-destructive. Many churches today could learn with profit from the example which the early church set in this regard. Over-worked pastoral staff and rival factions in the congregation are a familiar scenario. And sometimes the answer to the problem lies not in the prayer meeting, but in the business meeting.

5

Something Worth *Dying For*

Acts 6:8—8:1

Now Stephen, a man full of God's grace
and power, did great wonders and
miraculous signs among the people.
Opposition arose, however...These men
began to argue with Stephen, but they
could not stand up against his wisdom or
the Spirit by whom he spoke.

Acts 6:8—10

I DO NOT BELIEVE we can be sure we have something worth living for unless we are also ready to die for it. Of course, people may risk their lives for comparatively little; many a young hot-head lives dangerously simply for the thrill of gambling with death. That kind of recklessness is not real valour; the truly courageous person ventures his or her life thoughtfully and soberly, because something very important is at stake.

The story is told of two soldiers at the frontline, lying under their blankets, looking up at the stars one night, sleepless with the noise of exploding shells in their ears. 'What made you volunteer?' asks Jack of his comrade.

'Well,' replies Tom, 'I have no wife or children, and I love the excitement of war, so I joined up. What made you volunteer?'

'Well,' replied Jack, 'I've got a wife and children, and we love the peace of our home. That is why I joined.'

There is all the difference in the world between the motivation of those two. The one, a dare-devil who hazards his life because he has nothing to live for and the other, a hero, who hazards his life because he has something so precious, it is not only worth living for, it is worth dying for as well.

In this chapter we shall study Stephen, a young man of similar stamp. Unlike Jack, his commitment led not to a battle-front, but to a courtroom; not to the death of a soldier, but to that of a martyr. We do not know a great deal about him. We read that he was a man full of faith and the Holy Spirit (6:5), and that he did great wonders and miraculous signs among the people (6:8). He was obviously quite a remarkable Christian with an obvious supernatural charisma. But he does not seem to have been an intimidating personality, for we also read in chapter 6 verse 8 that he was full of grace as well as power, and in this context that word probably implies he was charming and attractive. We are even told in chapter 6 verse 18 that his accusers found him beaming at them like an angel.

Here was a man, then, in whom the Holy Spirit had done his distinctive work, producing authority without aloofness; winsomeness without wimpishness. And not surprisingly his potential was quickly recognised by the church. He was one of the seven men appointed to look after the church's welfare programme—a very responsible post. And as we indicated in the previous chapter, almost certainly that means he was a Hellenistic Jew, raised not in the Aramaic-speaking conservatism of Jerusalem, but in the much more cosmopolitan atmosphere of Greek culture. That is confirmed by the controversy in which Stephen found himself entangled. Opposition against him arose from a group of Jews called the Synagogue of the Freedmen, a title which suggests that they were descendants of former Roman slaves who had obtained their liberty. Luke tells us they came from imperial provinces in North Africa and Asia, so, like Stephen, they were unquestionably Hellenistic in culture. It is probable that there were a number of intellectuals among them, because the city of Alexandria which Luke mentions, was a famous centre of Jewish learning at this time. Indeed, it is quite likely that Saul of Tarsus, whom we shall meet a little later, belonged to this synagogue, since he was certainly a Roman citizen, and Tarsus was the chief city of Cilicia, which is also mentioned here.

No doubt Stephen got involved in debate with this rather sophisticated and elite group because, unlike the apostles, he spoke fluent Greek. And it is clear his opponents experienced great difficulty in contradicting his eloquence: 'They could not stand up against his wisdom, or the Spirit by which he spoke' (6:10).

And to their shame, being unable to confute him by argument, they resorted to intrigue and conspiracy. First, by engineering false testimony: 'They secretly persuaded some men to say, "We have heard Stephen speak words of blasphemy..."' (6:11). Then by formenting hostility among the general public and the authorities: 'They stirred up the people and the elders and the teachers of the law. They seized Stephen and brought him before the Sanhedrin' (6:12).

So, to cut a long story short, this radiant and remarkable young man ended his life later that very day under a hail of angry rocks, the first but by no means last Christian to fertilise the earth with his blood.

Why did this exemplary young man find himself the victim of such homicidal malice? Luke is clear that he was the victim of a shameful frame-up. It was obvious to anybody that there was nothing seditious or criminal about him. His only crime was that he got up the noses of these influential Jews of the Synagogue of the Freedmen; hardly a capital offence. And the penalty he suffered was almost certainly illegal, for Jewish courts at this time did not have the power to order a capital sentence without the approval of the Roman Governor. Stephen was not executed, he was lynched. His trial was a travesty of justice from start to finish. Why did it happen? Luke observes two factors which contributed towards the tragedy.

The silent sympathisers

> The apostles performed many miraculous signs and wonders among the people. And all the believers used to meet together in Solomon's Colonnade. No-one else dared join them, even though they were highly regarded by the people (5:12–13).

Some translators find this verse a little difficult because it seems to contradict the spirit of what follows where Luke speaks about many conversions: 'More and more men and women believed in the Lord' (5:14).

The situation is not really hard to imagine, however. The infant church was a popular and honoured movement, but the majority of the general public were not willing to express their support for it openly because they were scared. They were scared perhaps that they would not come up to the standard that this group demanded; after all, Ananias and Sapphira had come to a sticky end, just because they had told a lie at the church meeting. But more importantly they were scared of the authorities. Word was getting round that the Jewish Sanhedrin disapproved of Christianity. They had crucified its Master and now they had imprisoned Peter and John. Clearly, anyone who joined their number was likely to be putting his head in a noose. So they preferred to play safe. 'Christianity,' they said, 'is obviously an admirable thing, but we would rather not get involved personally.' They were content, like spectators at a football match, to applaud from the grandstand; sympathetic, but uncommitted.

That of course is the position of a great number of people in this world today. They respect the church and hold the Bible in reverence. They have a conscience perhaps about using the name of Christ blasphemously, particularly if a Christian is within earshot. They put their 50p in the Christian Aid envelope. If they go to hospital they certainly want 'Church of England' put on their notes. If the vicar comes to call, they give him a very polite cup of tea. But, much as they admire it, they do not want to identify closely with Christianity. I believe the reason for that is much the same as it was for the first-century people of Jerusalem: they too are scared. No doubt they have less cause to be so, for no one is going to persecute the average British citizen for becoming a Christian in the 1990s. But there are anxieties nevertheless—albeit less extreme—which do still deter those who are seriously drawn towards Christ; fear of ridicule, for instance. Nobody is going to lock us up, flog us, or execute us if we become Christians today, but mockery is still a real possibility. The crowd is a secure place to be. Being a Christian puts you in the public eye; it makes you stand out against the mass. It makes you different; it makes you identifiable. Old friends will point you out and whisper behind your back, 'What has come over old Fred? He has become very odd lately. Must be religious mania I reckon.' Most of us would prefer to keep out of the pillory by staying with the majority. Fear of ridicule keeps people uncommitted today, just as it did in Jerusalem.

Jesus anticipated as much when he talked about the cost of discipleship. Though the church charges no fee to become a member, it does not mean it is a cheap society to join. 'Take up your cross daily and follow me'. That is what Jesus says and it is a disturbingly expensive challenge. Many people, when they sit down and work out the cost, decide it is all too much of a gamble and they would prefer to play safe.

C.S. Lewis writes in one of his books how, as a child, when he had toothache he would refuse to complain to his mother because he knew that although she would give him an aspirin that would take the pain away, she would also take him to the dentist, and he was afraid of the dentist. 'Dentists,' he says, 'though they assured you they were doing it for your good, were painful places to visit. I know these dentists,' says Lewis, 'once they get you in their chair they start fiddling about with teeth that have not even started to hurt yet. You give them an inch and they take a mile.' That is the secret fear of many an uncommitted sympathiser with Christianity. He would quite like to be a Christian, and deep down in his soul he feels a need which he suspects Jesus could satisfy, but there are too many risks involved. So he stays safely on the sidelines of Christian experience as an onlooker, or an admirer, sometimes even as a patron, but never as a participant. Luke is surely right in suggesting that deep down there is cowardice in such lack of commitment.

They refuse to become Christians, not because they do not want to, but because they dare not. And the pusillanimous silent majority who thought that way in Jerusalem have to bear their share of blame for Stephen's death. They were on his side privately perhaps, but rather like passive witnesses at a mugging, they did not want to get involved, or to risk their own necks. They would rather let the innocent perish than identify themselves with the truth for which he stood. It was Edmund Burke who said that the triumph of evil in this world required nothing more than that good men do nothing.

The agnostic fence-sitter

This lack of commitment is highlighted again in the reaction of the influential Pharisee, Gamaliel. We meet him during yet another official interrogation of the apostles by the Jewish Council. This time there is pressure not just to imprison them, but to have them executed. It is then that, unexpectedly, Gamaliel stands to advise moderation.

> Men of Israel, consider carefully what you intend to do to these men. Some time ago Theudas appeared, claiming to be somebody, and about four hundred men rallied to him. He was killed, all his followers were dispersed, and it all came to nothing. After him, Judas the Galilean appeared in the days of the census and led a band of people in revolt. He too was killed, and all his followers scattered. Therefore, in the present case I advise you: Leave these men alone! Let them go! For if their purpose or activity is of human origin, it will fail. But if it is from God, you will not be able to stop these men; you will only find yourselves fighting against God (5:35–39).

We know from other contemporary Jewish sources that Gamaliel was one of the most outstanding scholars of his day. We would describe him today as a professor of theology. And on the surface his words do seem to exhibit a very scholarly wisdom. They even won a temporary respite from persecution for the Christians. The apostles, instead of being put to death, were flogged and given an official warning as a result of his counsel. And yet, I have to say that I have always been profoundly dissatisfied with Gamaliel's argument, and I am very far from being as impressed with him as many commentators seem to be. He makes, it seems to me, three fatal mistakes in this learned opinion which he expresses to his fellow lawyers in the Jewish judiciary; mistakes that are still being made today by people who, like him, want to maintain the detached indecisiveness of an open-minded agnostic when it comes to Christianity.

A fallacious comparison

The implication of the two comparisons made by Gamaliel is clear: Theudas and Judas were political extremists and he is suggesting that Christ belonged to the same category. 'This church of Jesus is just a religious cover for yet another anti-colonial, pseudo-messianic guerrilla organisation like all the others; it is nothing new.' This is a classic way in which scholars like Gamaliel, down through the ages, have again and again sought to evade giving serious consideration to Christianity. They put Jesus into a pigeon-hole with others whose causes have already been discredited. 'He was another reformer, another revolutionary, another philosopher, another guru. We know about such characters. We have dealt with them before.' The goal of such dismissive categorisation is always the same. Once Jesus is filed in such a pigeon-hole, he and his church can be conveniently ignored.

Well, Gamaliel was wrong about that. Jesus cannot be aligned with first-century freedom fighters. If he had taken the trouble to look at the evidence, he would have seen that straight away. By far the most disturbing thing about Jesus of Nazareth is that he does not fit into any pigeon-hole. Everything about him is unique. He cannot be set alongside a first-century Theudas or Judas any more than he can be set alongside a twentieth-century Che Guevara or Mahatma Ghandi. He is quite literally incomparable. You can call him a mad man if you like, but if that was so, he was quite exceptionally mad, for he claimed to be God in the flesh. You can call him a fraud if you like, but if that was so, he was the best con-man who ever lived, because he rose from the dead before many witnesses. Whatever he was, he was not like anybody else. Gamaliel's comparisons are invidious and misleading, grossly underestimating the riddle of Christ's person, and inviting a careless disregard of a man, who more than any other individual who has ever lived, demands our close attention.

A fallacious principle

> If their purpose or activity is of human origin, it will fail. But if it is from God, you will not be able to stop these men (5:38–39).

Now that sounds very enlightened and very spiritual. Indeed, Luke may even see a kind of unintended prophetic truth in it. But used in the way

Gamaliel is using it here it is a very dangerous criterion, for he is suggesting it is possible to judge whether a thing is right or wrong by its success. Such a principle may work in the world of business but it certainly will not do when it comes to making judgements on moral and spiritual issues. The Bible makes it plain that God's success stories often read like failures to the world, and Gamaliel knew that.

Consider the Old Testament stories with which he was so familiar. Abraham leaving wealthy Ur to become a nomad in the desert; Moses giving up a place in Pharaoh's palace to share affliction with a band of escaped slaves in the wilderness; Jeremiah languishing in a pit before the contempt of his fellow countrymen, or Nehemiah giving up a well-paid job in the civil service to build a wall round a ruin. These are not success stories. Gamaliel knew perfectly well that success is a very bad criterion of God's support. The whole point of this Christianity he was trying to dismiss so contemptuously is that its Founder succeeded precisely when he seemed to fail. For success in God's book is frequently invisible to human vision. Only faith that perceives the invisible and eternal dimensions of a situation can recognise the true success of God's servants, or the true failure of those who rebel against him. One dreads to imagine how many demons would have been canonised as saints if it were true that worldly success constitutes a stamp of divine approval. It is not as simple as that. For a Bible scholar of Gamaliel's stature to evade the message of Christianity by specious arguments of that sort was the height of irresponsibility.

A fallacious conclusion

> Therefore, in the present case I advise you: Leave
> these men alone! (5:38).

Commentators dispute Gamaliel's motives in
offering that cautionary advice. Some surmise that it
was borne of private sympathy; perhaps he was one
of those who entertained a sneaking regard for this
Christian movement, and secretly wanted to see it
prosper. That could have been so, but Luke gives no
hint in that direction. Others suggest it was borne of
political expediency; he was just speaking in the
coded theological language of Jewish diplomacy at
that time. 'Let the Romans handle these Christians as
they have every other Galilean zealot. Why should
we risk our popular standing among the people by
making martyrs of them?' Again, that is possible,
though Luke does not spell it out.

Personally, I think it best to interpret Gamaliel's
advice here as a piece of typical academic vacillation.
Trained as he was to see both sides of the argument,
he looked instinctively for a safe compromise,
nailing his colours firmly to the fence. Unwilling to
endorse or to contradict the Christians, he opted for a
policy of *laissez faire*. 'Let us see what happens. Leave
them alone,' he advises. But that is one thing no
intelligent or responsible person can possibly do
with Christians. If the apostolic message is true, it is
the most important thing that has ever happened in
the history of the world. If it is false, it is the most
outrageous lie ever perpetrated on the general public. You cannot adopt a non-committal position. The
claims of Jesus Christ demand a verdict.

There have been many such men down the years

who have similarly sat on the fence and refused to back either side in spite of the fact that momentous issues were at stake. Gamaliel was what in pre-war British politics they called an 'appeaser'; the sort of moral invertebrate who made Munich such a farce by looking for a compromise when what was needed was decision. Like Erasmus in the sixteenth century or Thomas Huxley in the nineteenth century, he is a scholarly 'don't know'. There are still thousands of them around, defending their agnosticism by calling it 'open-mindedness'. Of course, there are times when open-mindedness is a virtue, but there are also issues over which such non-alignment is indefensible. As John F. Kennedy once said, 'The hottest places in hell are reserved for those who in times of great moral crisis, maintain their neutrality.'

When it comes to the Christian gospel, of course, we may well pass through periods of uncertainty when we are trying to find our way through doubt. But it is not possible to defend agnosticism as a permanent habit of mind. The issues are too important for that. When it comes to Christianity, as G.K. Chesterton once said, 'The object of opening the mind is the same as that of opening the mouth: to shut it again on something solid.' Jesus himself refused to accept a neutral verdict. 'He who is not for me is against me,' he said. He left no limbo for agnostics to hide in on the Day of Judgement. To be open-minded about him is like being open-minded about whether the house is on fire. Such questions do not admit agnosticism. We either believe or we don't, for there is nothing in between. We are either living our lives on the basis that Jesus *is* God risen from the dead and coming again in glory, or we are not. To try to avoid taking sides on that is simply to abdicate responsibility for one's own life and destiny.

That is what makes Gamaliel's indecision particularly culpable. He may have gained a temporary reprieve for the apostles by this policy of deliberate indecision, but what he did was in fact to leave the field wide open to others, like the Synagogue of the Freedmen, who lacked his distaste for violence, who had less confidence in divine providence and who certainly did not display his propensity towards toleration. If we are not passionately committed to the vindication of truth, then we must bear part of the blame when those who are passionately committed to its denial achieve their purpose. Gamaliel could no more evade his complicity in Stephen's death with his open-minded agnosticism, than could Pilate cleanse his heart of the stain of Christ's blood by washing his hands. 'They covered their ears and, yelling at the top of their voices, they all rushed at him, dragged him out of the city and began to stone him' (7:57–58).

There were plenty of people in Jerusalem sympathetic to Christianity who could have stepped in to stop it, but cowardice kept them on the sidelines as uncommitted observers. There were scholars like Gamaliel, who knew that such violence was counterproductive and unnecessary. He could have wielded his authority to stop it at a stroke, but he preferred the aloof academic detachment of an open-minded agnostic. And so the advocates of violence had their way. If you had asked them why they were picking up stones and throwing them at this young man they would undoubtedly have said they were serving God by executing a heretic, as the law of Moses told them to do.

That perhaps is the deepest irony of all. For it was precisely Stephen's argument in his great defence speech that the era of the Jewish state with its theocratic constitution and its executions for heresy was passing away. The messianic kingdom had come and that was a kingdom of changed hearts. Hearts cannot be changed by coercion. Threats of violence may intimidate, but they cannot regenerate. Stephen understood that. The kingdom of God is not advanced by the kinds of means these fanatics were trying to use. Indeed, in the paradoxical economy of the kingdom of God, the way God's purpose is advanced is not by killing, but by dying; not by executions, but by martyrdoms. Here was a man who had something worth living for, and we know he had something worth living for, because he was prepared to die for it.

Silent sympathisers and indecisive agnostics like Gamaliel may live longer, but they live less purposefully too. We shall see in the next chapter that brave Stephen probably accomplished more for the extension of the kingdom of God by his death, than he ever could have done by his life.

An Evangelist Is Born

Acts 8:1–40

Philip went down to a city in Samaria and proclaimed the Christ there. When the crowds heard and saw the miraculous signs he did, they all paid close attention to what he did. With shrieks, evil spirits came out of many, and many paralytics and cripples were healed. So there was great joy in that city.

Acts 8:4–8

An Evangelist Is Born

'**P**HILOSOPHERS HAVE merely interpreted the world in different ways. The real task is to change it.' Those are the words of Karl Marx, a man who had little time for ivory tower academics or armchair dreamers. He was a revolutionary, and 'Revolution,' he said, 'requires action.' You do not change the world just by theorising. You have to get up and do something. The big question is: what?

The revolutionary praxis of Marx and his disciples, as we have witnessed in many places in the last 150 years, is one of violence, class conflict and political authoritarianism. That such tactics have changed the world no one can question, but whether they have succeeded in changing the world for the better is much more debatable. The recent collapse of the Soviet Union is not particularly encouraging in that respect. We can surely ask whether there is not some better way to change the world; some methodology of revolution which is superior to guns and bombs?

As we have seen already, the Book of Acts believes that there is indeed an alternative: the revolution of Jesus. In the very first chapter, the risen Jesus set out his agenda of world conquest: 'In Jerusalem, and in all Judea and Samaria, and to the ends of the earth'

(1:8). Just like a stone dropped into a pond, so the ripples of his impact would penetrate the whole globe in ever-increasing circles. Christianity is emphatically not a philosophy that is content just to interpret the world. Jesus, like Marx, is a revolutionary who intends to *change* the world. In this chapter we catch a glimpse of the way in which he intends to do that; not with guns and bombs, but by *evangelism*.

The beginning of evangelism

> On that day a great persecution broke out against the church at Jerusalem, and all except the apostles were scattered throughout Judea and Samaria (8:1).

Up until this point Christianity has been a highly localised phenomenon. All the Christians have been concentrated in Jerusalem. But now the process of expansion which Jesus had predicted was about to commence. The believers are scattered throughout Judea and Samaria, just the very places he mentioned when he defined the church's missionary agenda. And, ironically, what triggers this movement outwards is the persecution consequent upon the death of Stephen. Notice the word Luke uses: they were 'scattered', he says. It is the word you would use of broadcasting seed on the soil.

The Jewish authorities, in their attempt to lance the boil of Christian heresy that was brewing in their midst, only succeed in spreading the germ further afield. Instead of halting the church's growth, they actually encourage it. For this was a church that had learned to talk about its faith courageously. And now: 'Those who had been scattered preached the word wherever they went' (8:4).

Tertullian, in his great apology for the Christian faith, challenged the Roman authorities of his day: 'Kill us, torture us, condemn us, grind us to dust. The more you mow us down, the more we grow, for the seed of the church is the blood of the Christians.' In Stephen's case, his blood was indeed the signal for the next stage in the expansion of the church. In the remaining chapters of this book we are going to see how Luke traces the various strands of that centrifugal explosion of missionary activity. And he begins by focusing on the pioneering activities of one man who single-handedly demonstrates the two things a Christian evangelist must be: a church planter and a soul winner.

A church planter

Philip went down to a city in Samaria and proclaimed the Christ there (8:5).

Samaria was a kind of halfway house between the Jews and the world at large. The people there were of mixed blood, but they had a good deal in common with the Jews, and that is why they could understand Philip's preaching. He preached Jesus as the Christ, the Messiah. An outright Gentile would not have been able to make sense of that, but the Samaritans could because they had a background of Old Testament knowledge. They too were expecting a Messiah.

There is clearly wisdom in God's providence here. He begins the church's exposure to the world outside with a group of people who, though not identical, were culturally related to those first Christians. He chose the appropriate man too. For Philip was a Greek-speaking Jew, one of those like Stephen appointed by the apostles to help in the administration of the church (see 6:5). We have already commented on the fact that such Hellenistic Jews were more open to the outside world than their more conservative Aramaic-speaking cousins who had spent all their lives in Jerusalem or the surrounding area.

We are not told what decided Philip to preach to these Samaritans. Was it just an impulse? A desire for adventure? We do not know how far he had thought through the implications of his evangelism. But we do know from the evidence of his speech (7:1–53) that his colleague Stephen was a theologian of considerable insight. He had worked out that the kingdom of God was not going to remain tied around the ceremony of the Jerusalem temple for ever. God had bigger plans than that. It was his attempt to communicate these insights in his preaching which so offended the Jewish establishment (see 6:13–14).

Perhaps Philip had taken on board Stephen's theology and was keen to work out its practical implications. We can't be sure. But for whatever reason, Philip broke new ground by deciding to preach to the Samaritans. And there was a most astonishing response to his experiment: 'When the crowds heard Philip and saw the miraculous signs he did, they all paid close attention to what he said. With shrieks, evil spirits came out of many, and many paralytics and cripples were healed. So there was great joy in that city' (8:6–8).

This is an absolutely critical transition point in this Book of Acts. Here is a major breakthrough.

Non-Jews are for the first time responding to the gospel.

Not surprisingly Philip's evangelistic success caused some consternation in the parent church back in Jerusalem: 'When the apostles in Jerusalem heard that Samaria had accepted the word of God, they sent Peter and John to them' (8:14).

What was the reason for this sudden delegation of spiritual heavy-weights? Clearly the apostles were disturbed by what had happened. Philip's action raised all kinds of new questions which the church had not faced before.

Philip, you see, had no real authority to do what he had done. As we said earlier, the church at this point had not sat down and said, 'Now is the time for us to send out missionaries. Now is the time for us to start our process of planting churches around the world.' It had just happened spontaneously. Though the apostles were excited to hear of the success which Philip had experienced in taking the gospel to the Samaritans, a dangerous precedent had also been set. Up to this point there had only been one church— the one in Jerusalem. But now there was another congregation out there in Samaria. How was that new Christian community to be related to the church in Jerusalem? Was Jerusalem to be identified as the organisational centre of the Christian church? Would unity be maintained by requiring all Christians to conform to the discipline of some central ideological agency? If not, how would the church be delivered from disintegration into all kinds of unrelated sects and cults, as these hot-headed young Christians, scattered throughout the world, began to do elsewhere what Philip had done in Samaria?

In a fascinating and unexpected twist of events, it

is God himself who signals the answer to this vital question of missionary policy.

> When they [Peter and John] arrived, they prayed for them that they might receive the Holy Spirit, because the Holy Spirit had not yet come upon any of them; they had simply been baptised into the name of the Lord Jesus. Then Peter and John placed their hands on them, and they received the Holy Spirit (8:15–17).

These verses have been widely used in pentecostal circles in a way that misses the real thrust of the incident. The whole point is that the Holy Spirit was not usually withheld from new believers. By doing so in this case God was signalling that there was something irregular in what had happened. The new church which Philip founded possessed no direct link with the apostles, and hence no conscious dependence upon their authoritative testimony regarding the foundations of the Christian faith.

By engineering events so that it was only when Peter and John arrived that the manifestation of the Holy Spirit was bestowed (probably in a manner similar to that on the Day of Pentecost), God was ensuring two things.

First, he was confirming in the minds of the apostles themselves that this undoubtedly was a real work of God, a continuation of the pentecostal shower which they themselves had experienced. That confirmation would be important when they got back to Jerusalem and had to explain what was going on in Samaria to conservative Jewish Christians who were suspicious of Philip's venture.

Even more importantly, however, it made quite clear to the Samaritan believers themselves that Peter and John were in a different category from Philip. They were apostles, and God authorised them in a way in which he did not authorise Philip.

An ancient creed of the church says, 'I believe in one catholic and apostolic church.' What do we mean by that adjective 'apostolic'? What does Paul mean when he says the church is 'built on the foundation of the apostles' (Eph 2:20)? What is the significance of that passage in the Book of Revelation which speaks of the New Jerusalem being built on twelve foundations, inscribed with the names of the twelve apostles (Rev 21:14)?

Some people suggest that an apostolic church must be able to trace its origin through a chain of bishops, who derive from the apostles themselves. But there is no evidence, either historical or biblical, that the apostles appointed any such successors to themselves. Some people say that an apostolic church is one in which the miraculous gifts of the early church are still evident. But that will not do either, because there have been long centuries where such charismata were completely unknown, and it cannot be true there was no apostolic church on earth during that time.

No, the answer to this question is implicit here. An apostolic church is one which consciously recognises the distinctive authority of apostolic teaching. That is why Peter and John had to come to Samaria. Philip was a great evangelist, but he was not an apostle.

There were definite criteria by which apostles were identified, the most important being that they had received their understanding of the Christian message direct from Jesus himself. They were first-hand witnesses both of his resurrection and of his instruction. If the efforts of evangelists like Philip were not to result in the gospel becoming distorted as it was preached in new cultures, then it was vital that the unique role of the apostles be recognised from the start in any new Christian church that was planted. This God achieved in Samaria by his startling demonstration of the special authority which Peter and John wielded.

For us today then, being an apostolic church has nothing to do with bishops and charismatic gifts. It has everything to do with where we get our doctrine from. For us, apostolic authority now resides in the New Testament—the books and letters which preserve for us the apostles' teaching.

We do not have a succession of infallible bishops or of inspired prophets, but a deposit of inspired and infallible apostolic truth. That is why, when Paul writes to Timothy at the very end of his life, and talks about what is going to happen after he is dead, he does not say, 'Timothy, I am going to die soon. You must look around for some apostolic successor or charismatic prophet who can continue to define the doctrine of the church as I have for you.' Nor does he appoint Timothy to such a role. What he says is, 'Timothy, you have to keep a firm hold on the pattern of sound words which you have heard from me. And you must communicate that pattern of sound words to the next generation of Christians without distortion' (see 2 Timothy 1). True apostolic succession is not a perpetuation of personal authority either by episcopal office or charismatic endowment. It is the ongoing communication of this deposit of the apostolic gospel once and for all delivered to the saints and passed on from generation to generation.

Notice carefully what the apostles did in Samaria:

'When they had testified and proclaimed the word of the Lord, Peter and John returned to Jerusalem preaching the gospel in many Samaritan villages' (8:25).

They recognised that this was an authentic church by the fact that it had received the Holy Spirit just as they had. And, having passed on their distinctive first-hand and authoritative knowledge of the events and message of the gospel, they went home. They did not set up an office. They did not attempt any kind of organisational bond between Jerusalem and Samaria. They seem to have been perfectly content to know that this church shared the same gospel, the same Holy Spirit and the same baptism that they did, and that was all the unity they required. Other than that, they left this new church to conduct its own affairs.

That is something we find happening again and again in the Book of Acts. In Acts 14, at the end of his first missionary journey, Paul appoints elders in each of the churches he has planted, and with prayer and fasting commits them to the Lord in whom they put their trust. Then he sails away. At the end of his second missionary journey in Acts 20, speaking to the elders of the Ephesian church, he says, 'Guard yourselves and all the flock of which the Holy Spirit has made you overseers. Be shepherds of the church of God, which he bought with his own blood' (20:28), and then again he gets into a ship and goes home.

There was no attempt on the part of the apostles, then, to try to maintain church unity around the world by any kind of bureaucratic control. It would have been very easy for Peter and John and the other apostles to attempt such organisational unity in their well-intentioned desire to protect these new churches from heresy. They might well have taken the attitude of an over-protective parent: 'Oh, you are far too young to be trusted with independence.' They were very familiar with such paternalistic government, after all. The Roman Empire was built upon a strategy of centralised control. But they did not copy the imperialistic structures of Rome. The new churches the evangelists planted were bound to one another by ties of affection and fellowship, but each one looked after its own affairs.

Within a matter of a few centuries, the church had abandoned that radical policy. The church became an empire, centralised like the Roman Empire in Rome, and began to exercise the same kind of hierarchical organisation. Not until after the European Reformation did anybody again seriously suggest that local churches should be independent of one another. But independent churches are the only churches the New Testament knows anything about. And that independency was a major factor in the extraordinary flexibility which the early church demonstrated in contextualising itself into totally novel cultural situations.

The vast majority of churches in this world today are ruled through the tutelage of bureaucratic bodies external to themselves. That body may be a denominational head office or a bishop's palace; it may be a foreign missionary society or a civil government. It may even be the Vatican. But to the extent that the church is dependent on such a body, it is victim to paternalism. Well meaning and benevolent, maybe, but paternalism nevertheless. Such paternalism is without New Testament warrant. Apostolic churches share the same New Testament gospel and the same Holy Spirit—but they are not part of a single organisation.

The early church did not have a power complex. It was building a spiritual kingdom—not a political empire. That is a lesson we need to rediscover in our church planting.

A soul winner

> Now an angel of the Lord said to Philip, 'Go south to the road—the desert road—that goes down from Jerusalem to Gaza.' So he started out, and on his way he met an Ethiopian eunuch, an important official in charge of all the treasury of Candace, queen of the Ethiopians. This man had gone to Jerusalem to worship, and on his way home was sitting in his chariot reading the Book of Isaiah the prophet. The Spirit told Philip, 'Go to that chariot and stay near it.'
>
> Then Philip ran up to the chariot and heard the man reading Isaiah the prophet. 'Do you understand what you are reading?' Philip asked (8:26–30).

It did not take a great imagination to realise that if God was willing for Samaritans to become Christians, it was quite possible he intended the gospel to go even further. And, once again, it was Philip that God used to make the next breakthrough. This Ethiopian was not a Jew or a Samaritan. He was not even a proselyte to Judaism, for as a eunuch the Old Testament law excluded him from the Jewish community. But this man was certainly interested in the Jewish faith, for we find him returning from Jerusalem with a piece of the Bible in his hands. He is an example of a Gentile God-fearer. There were many such people in the first century—unwilling or unable to submit to circumcision, but deeply sympathetic to biblical religion. In reaching out to him, Philip is breaching yet another critical boundary in the spread of the gospel. And in doing so he provides a very beautiful example of what one-to-one personal evangelism involves. If you want to know how to win somebody for Christ, Philip here is a very good model to follow.

Be sensitive

Notice first his sensitivity to God's prompting. Luke records that an angel of the Lord told him to go down to Gaza. We will not always have angels telling us to do things like that, but we must remember that Philip was being instructed to do something revolutionary. For the first time, the gospel was en route to a person who did not belong in any way to the Old Testament covenant people of God. So it is to be expected perhaps that God would provide an unusually clear directive. Even if we enjoy no such angelic visitation, however, we will sometimes experience similar prompting, as in fact seems to have happened to Philip himself when he got a little closer to his target: 'The Spirit told Philip, "Go to that chariot and stay near it" ' (8:29).

I do not think that we need to believe this was necessarily an audible voice; he may simply have felt an inward compulsion that he recognised to be divine in origin. Many of us have had experiences like that. And it is important that we are sensitive to such divine guidance. For the evangelist is not to button-hole everybody he encounters with belligerent enquiries about their spiritual state. He has to be tactful. Conversion is the Spirit's work. We must see ourselves as collaborators with him in identifying those people he wants us to talk to, because we do not have the power to manipulate anybody into becoming a Christian. Some who are excessively keen to win new Christians through their personal witness are prone to produce spiritual abortions because they lack that sensitivity. Philip shows commendable discernment here as he listens for the voice of God.

Be prepared for inconvenience

Secondly, it is worth noting that Philip had to be prepared for a certain amount of inconvenience to be used by God in this way: 'Go south to the road—the desert road—that goes down from Jerusalem to Gaza' (8:26).

This meant for Philip a journey of at least sixty miles, and though there is a hint (8:39) that Philip may have had some supernatural assistance for his return, he does not seem to have had any help in getting down there. It was a long way on a hot dusty road. Not a place we would choose to go on wild goose-chases, particularly during an enormously successful campaign such as Philip was enjoying in Samaria.

If we are going to be evangelists, however, sometimes we must be prepared for inconvenience of that sort. Stopping what we are doing suddenly, visiting unpleasant surroundings, receiving telephone calls in the middle of the night, making tiring and perhaps fruitless journeys. We may face all of these if we are sensitive to what God wants us to do in winning others for Christ.

Overcome prejudice, nerves and embarrassment

One thing that is certainly true of Philip is that he was willing to overcome personal prejudice. This fellow was first of all an Ethiopian, which meant that Philip had to overcome a certain amount of ethnic prejudice. He was very probably black. There was also a class barrier between them, for he was a government minister, an important civil servant, and Philip by comparison was a nobody. Imagine some top brass from an embassy driving down Whitehall in his chauffeur-driven Rolls, when some upstart on a bicycle draws alongside at the traffic lights and starts to talk to him through the open window. It would require a bit of nerve!

This man, however, was not just a foreign diplomat, he was a eunuch, and for a sensitive Jew that represented a very special embarrassment. Jews had been taught from time immemorial to have great distaste for this kind of sexual mutilation. Maybe the distaste some feel in the presence of an obvious homosexual provides a contemporary clue to how Philip might have reacted to this encounter. But Philip had to overcome all his natural awkwardness as we shall too if we are going to be used as evangelists. We must be willing for God to allow us to speak to some pretty odd people to whom we would not normally think of talking.

Be alert to opportunity

It is tempting to speculate about why this Ethiopian had purchased this particular volume from the religious bookshop in Jerusalem before he set off home. I have a theory about that based upon a rather lovely verse in Isaiah 56 which I am sure was in this scroll. It reads: 'Let not any eunuch complain, "I am only a dry tree."...To the eunuchs who...hold fast to my covenant—to them I will give within my temple and its walls a memorial and a name better than sons and daughters' (Is 56:3–5). That is a promise that in the messianic age the old ban that excluded eunuchs from the people of God would be revoked. It must have meant a lot to this fellow. He admired the Jewish religion and wanted to be part of it. But as things stood, he was excluded. God's hand of providence was at work, however, because he could not purchase Isaiah 56 without also purchasing Isaiah 53. And while reading his new volume, he had been interested in that earlier passage: 'He was led like a sheep to the slaughter, and as a lamb before the shearer is silent so he did not open his mouth. In his humiliation he was deprived of justice. Who can speak of his descendants? For his life was taken from the earth' (Acts 8:32–33).

'What is it all about?' he asks Philip. 'Tell me, who is the prophet talking about, himself or somebody else?' Philip could scarcely have asked for a more obvious opportunity. Not all evangelistic conversations will present themselves quite as easily as that, but opportunity is always there, and needs to be seized when it arises. Notice the evangelist's discretion in seeking such an opening. 'Do you understand what you are reading?' (8:30) he asks. He does not start the conversation by challenging the eunuch, but by asking a question. That is a useful hint. Asking polite questions is a more fruitful overture than offering opinions or advice. See how well received Philip's initiative is: ' "How can I," he said, "unless someone explains it to me?" ' (8:31).

Use the Bible

'Who is the prophet talking about, himself or someone else?' Then Philip began with that very passage of Scripture and told him the good news about Jesus (8:34–35).

To be invited by a non-Christian to have a Bible study after a thirty-seconds conversation is unusual. But sooner or later every evangelist must seek to turn his listener's attention to its pages. And then we need Philip's skill in biblical interpretation as well.

Isaiah 53 is a notoriously cryptic passage of the Old Testament. It describes a Suffering Servant who dies for the sins of the people of God, but whose identity is left a mystery. Scholars even today argue about its meaning. Philip, however, knew the key to interpreting such Old Testament prophecies. He drew a line from it to Jesus. If we are going to be evangelists, then we too must have sufficient biblical knowledge to be able to interpret the text in such a way. There are some folk, I am afraid, who try to evangelise without a Bible, who offer spiritual counsel without biblical authority, and spiritual experience without biblical foundation. That is not real evangelism for the 'evangel' is the gospel, and it is only the Bible which can unfold that gospel to us and to our hearers with any reliability.

Have confidence in God's providence
Philip brings this strategic new convert to the point of baptism: 'As they travelled along the road, they came to some water and the eunuch said, "Look, here is water. Why shouldn't I be baptised?" ' (8:36).

Why not indeed? Some later texts include Philip's answer: 'If you believe with all your heart, you may,' and the eunuch's answer: 'I believe that Jesus Christ is the Son of God.' While these may not have been part of Luke's original document, it is clearly implicit in the passage that this man had become a believer and should be baptised as a result.

Some Christians fight shy of recommending baptism to a new believer so candidly. Today, unfortunately, baptism is an issue of controversy among Christians, and we do not feel so secure in taking a firm line. But this eunuch seems to have known either from what Philip said or from his previous knowledge of Christian practice that baptism was the next step. So with the minimum of delay, he was immersed: 'When they came up out of the water, the Spirit of the Lord suddenly took Philip away' (8:39).

We might be tempted to say that it was highly irregular for Philip to leave the man in the lurch like that. He should have done something about follow-up, surely? At the very least he should have sent his name to the pastor in Addis Ababa or given him a copy of John's Gospel to read in his quiet times. But, unfortunately, there was no pastor in Ethiopia and John had not written his Gospel yet. No, God had decided that in this case Philip would be just a link in the chain. Sometimes that will be the way it is for us too. We can't always plant a church. Sometimes we have to be content simply to win an individual and leave his integration into the Christian community in God's hands.

The Ethiopian Orthodox Church claims it was founded by this man. Certainly God had begun a work in him, and as a baptised member of the church of Jesus Christ we may be sure he would find fellowship eventually in his home city. Philip had to trust the Holy Spirit to acontinue the good work that he had begun. For the ripples were spreading fast now, and God had more evangelistic work for him to do elsewhere.

7

A *Missionary Is Converted*

'Who are you, Lord?' Saul asked.
'I am Jesus, whom you are persecuting,'
he replied. 'Now get up and go into the
city, and you will be told what you must
do.'

Acts 9:5–6

JOHN BUNYAN said he wanted to tell the cows in the fields about it, he was so full of joy. Charles Spurgeon tells us he danced all the way home after it happened to him. Blaise Pascal, a French philosopher of the seventeenth century, speaks of time seeming to stand still for a whole two hours while he was completely lost in ecstasy. There is no doubt about it, Christian conversion can be a stupendously overwhelming experience.

But it is not always so. For some, who have struggled for a long while against doubt, the final step of commitment can seem almost an anti-climax, a sigh of relief rather than a whoop of joy. One thinks of C.S. Lewis who wrote in his autobiography, 'I gave in and admitted that God was God, perhaps that night the most dejected convert in all Christendom.' And some, particularly those from a strong Christian family background, seem to slide quietly and gently into a personal relationship with God with almost no emotional upheaval at all. John Wesley, for instance, tells how he was listening one evening to an exposition of the letter to the Romans being given in London, when he felt his heart 'strangely warmed';

nothing more euphoric than that, but it was enough to transform his life.

And that, of course, is the real test. Mystical ecstasies, emotional crises or mind-blowing raptures of all sorts may accompany a conversion, or they may not. Their presence does not authenticate the experience, and their absence does not belie it. For conversion is not fundamentally a particular kind of religious feeling. Conversion, as the word itself suggests, is fundamentally a turning around, a change of moral and spiritual direction. You can tell whether someone has been converted, not so much by the account they give of what happened to them at the turning point, as by the evidence their life provides of such a real moral and spiritual reversal.

In this chapter we shall look at what must be one of the most dramatic conversions of all time. Paul's encounter with the risen Jesus on the Damascus Road. Everybody has heard of it, and for many it is a paradigm of what conversion ought to be. Some speak of their own 'Damascus Road experience' as if this was the acme of spiritual privilege. There can be no doubt that Paul's conversion was an absolutely crucial event, and the Book of Acts underlines that by recounting it no less than three times. It is quite clear that in the mind of author Luke, Paul's conversion was a key moment in the history of the early church. If it had not happened, the growth of Christianity in the first century would have been vastly less prolific than it was. But that is precisely the point. We know that Paul was truly converted on the Damascus Road, not because of the heavenly light that enveloped him, or the supernatural voice that spoke to him, but because of the radical change that came over him. It is the contrast in this man, before and after, that is the real miracle. And it is *only* in that respect that his Damascus Road experience is a model for all Christian conversion.

The vital question we have to ask ourselves is not, 'Have I had a dramatic spiritual crisis like Paul's?' but, 'Does the evidence of my life today prove that, whatever I may have been in the past, I am today one who calls Jesus Christ "Lord" and really means it?' A person who can answer that in the affirmative is converted, no matter how unspectacular his spiritual experience may seem by comparison with Paul's. And a person who cannot, no matter how many decisions or commitments he may testify to, is unconverted. The test is not, 'Have supernatural events happened around me?' but, 'Has a supernatural change happened within me?'

Let us study that change as Paul illustrates it.

The person he was

> Meanwhile, Saul was still breathing out murderous threats against the Lord's disciples. He went to the high priest and asked him for letters to the synagogues in Damascus, so that if he found any there who belonged to the Way, whether men or women, he might take them as prisoners to Jerusalem (Acts 9:1–2).

In case you are confused on the point, 'Saul' is the original Jewish name of the man we later know as 'Paul'. He probably took the Latin alias 'Paulus' to enhance his acceptability in Gentile society. But at this stage in his career, such a concession would have been unthinkable. He was a fanatical Judaist and determined to eradicate these heretic Christians. There is something quite ferocious about the way

Luke describes his homicidal mood. He talks about him 'destroying the church' (8:3), using a rare word which conveys the idea of grievously damaging a human body, much as a wild animal might do. Indeed, there is something bestial about the ruthlessness with which he ferrets the Christians out, violently invading the privacy of their homes in order to seize and incarcerate them. If they fled he gave them no peace. He would pursue them all the way to Syria if necessary. He was convinced that the world must be purged of the Christian plague before it was irreparably infected by it.

Unlike his tutor, Gamaliel, Rabbi Saul was not prepared to play some cynical, cautious waiting game. His heart burned with passionate fanaticism and only blood would satisfy his obsessional hatred. He wanted these Christians dead. Men or women, it made no difference. No gentler treatment would suffice, for such vermin must be exterminated, or breeding at the prodigious rate that they were, they would over-run the whole world. So at least Saul, I am sure, was telling himself, as he set out along that long and dusty road to Damascus. Imagine him tapping his saddle-bags with smug satisfaction. He had letters from the High Priest, arrest warrants on capital charges. It was a privilege to be charged with such a task. With top-level official backing, his inquisition would be irresistible. The Christians in Damascus would not have a chance; he would nip their little heresy in the bud. The purity of the Jewish faith was safe in his hands.

If this was so, however, why did he feel so uneasy? What were these strange stabs of misgiving that kept challenging his heart? What he was doing was right; it was God's will. The highest authorities in his religion agreed with him about that. So how come he was suffering these qualms of guilt? There is no doubt that he was troubled in this way, for in one of the later accounts of his conversion, Paul himself testifies to a sentence on the lips of the risen Jesus which Luke omits here in his earlier account, but which unambiguously confirms that a fierce inner debate was raging inside the man: 'Saul, Saul, why do you persecute me? It is hard for you to kick against the goads' (26:14).

Like a stubborn mule, then, Saul of Tarsus was deliberately resisting the prodding of inner conviction. His assured exterior concealed a besieged and divided heart.

It is often the case of course that irrational hostility is a barrier erected to defend our threatened security. As Jung the psychologist observes, fanaticism is almost always found in individuals who are trying to compensate for secret doubts. Saul may have looked self-confident in his anti-Christian militancy, but inwardly he was at war with himself, desperately trying to silence the secret assaults of his conscience, and becoming all the more militant and aggressive as he did so. Only heaven could discern it though and see how hard it was for him to resist the goads.

We learn, you see, from Paul's own later correspondence (see Romans 7 and Philippians 3) that for all his pharisaical orthodoxy, he was at the deepest level of his personal honesty a very discontented man. The religion of Moses, which he had followed so assiduously from his youth, had not satisfied his soul. It made him feel sinful, but offered him no real sense of pardon; it made him aware of his sinful nature, but offered him no power to resist temptation. As a result, in spite of all his painstaking efforts to keep the law of God, he had never enjoyed ease of conscience or felt real moral victory. He was constantly beset with introspection, self-accusation and guilt. Though an impeccable Jew, he knew himself privately to be corrupt and dirty in God's sight. For all his prayers he did not really know God, and no amount of moral endeavour could instil the warmth and spontaneity he wanted into his relationship with God. His was a frigid religion of smug self-righteousness and sanctimonious pride which left his heart empty, longing for some assurance that this God he served accepted him, valued him, wanted him and loved him. He had no peace and no joy, and the more zealous he became in the pursuit of his religion, the more spiritually frustrated he felt. As he puts it in his letter to the Romans: 'The law of Moses may be holy and good but to a sinful man like me it just spelt death and damnation.' Could it be, then, that these Christians were really onto something when they talked about the forgiveness of sins and the power of the Holy Spirit? Deep down that was what Saul longed to experience.

There was another source of unease hammering at his confidence too. In spite of himself, he could not help being impressed by the testimony of these Christians he was persecuting. The first time we read about Saul is as a junior member of the Jewish Council, when he had cast his vote against Stephen (see 7:58—8:1). Though he quite clearly gave consent to his death, it is noticeable that Saul took no active part in the brutal execution that followed. We read that those who prepared to stone Stephen 'laid their clothes at Saul's feet'. He was implicated, then, but interestingly he did not lift a violent hand himself against that saintly young man. He just watched as amid the avalanche of rocks that rained down upon him, Stephen looked up to heaven and saw the risen Christ standing at the right hand of God and said, 'Lord, do not hold this sin against them.'

As a Pharisee, Saul honoured the martyrs of the Jewish faith. He knew of many brave men who had given their lives courageously to preserve unsullied and uncompromised the ancient religion of his fore-fathers. But he had never seen or heard of anyone who had died like that, so generous to his torturers and so confident of the life to come. Had he been in Jerusalem during Passover to witness the crucifixion of Jesus? If so, he could scarcely fail to observe the uncanny similarity between the way that Stephen and his Master had died. If only these Christians would put up a fight! This habit they had of turning the other cheek made him feel so bitterly ashamed of his complicity in their suffering—the very idea of praying for your executors in your dying breath. It was outrageous!

Could it be that Jesus of Nazareth really was still alive? Could his Spirit really be inside these disciples of his, as they said, teaching them to love in the same way that he had loved?

Such were the questions that tortured Saul's mind as he journeyed along that lonely and quiet Damascus Road. Perhaps there are questions that assail you too. For Saul was not the first, nor will he be the last person to put up a front of antagonism against Christianity, while inwardly finding himself being drawn irresistibly towards it.

Is it perhaps the case that you too feel inwardly frustrated by your failings? Have you too been impressed by Christians you have met? Hard as you try to resist the idea, are you also kicking against the goads? I know that feeling very well because as a young man I did it myself for at least eighteen months. As an avowed atheist there was no way I could allow myself to be converted. I told myself that it would be a monumental climb-down. Paul was trapped in that way too by his intellectual pride. What would his colleagues in the Theology Department at Jerusalem say when he went and told them, 'I have been converted to Christianity'? You can just imagine the scorn. But more than that, there was his moral pride too. To admit that he, Saul the Pharisee, needed God's grace—it was inconceivable. To admit that all those years of religious diligence had been wasted effort. To throw away all that carefully constructed reputation for holiness, and all for the sake of a crucified Galilean—it did not bear thinking about.

There are times when no matter how inwardly convicted we are, it is far easier to continue to tell lies than to face the appalling humiliation of admitting that we have been wrong. But Christ can be infuriatingly persistent.

> I fled him down the night, and down the days,
> I fled him down the arches of the years.
> I fled him down the labyrinthine ways
> of my own mind, and in the midst of tears
> I hid from him, and under running laughter
> Up vistaed hopes I sped, and shot
> precipitated down titanic glooms
> of chasmed fears, from those strong feet
> that followed, followed after.
> But with unhurrying chase
> and unperturbed pace,
> deliberate speed, majestic instancy
> they beat, and a voice beat

more instant than the feet.
All things betray thee who betrayest me.

So Francis Thomson describes the futility of flight from the Hound of Heaven. He will not go away. In moments of silence he will slip through. Turn from the path for fear of meeting him, and at the end of the lane he will still be there, waiting for you, even as he was there waiting for Saul of Tarsus on the Damascus Road.

The person he met

As he neared Damascus on his journey, suddenly a light from heaven flashed around him. He fell to the ground and heard a voice say to him, 'Saul, Saul, why do you persecute me?'
'Who are you, Lord?' Saul asked.
'I am Jesus, whom you are persecuting,' he replied (9:3–5).

Paul on one occasion called this encounter a 'vision' (26:19), but it is important to realise this was not a private mystical experience on Paul's part. If you put the three accounts of this remarkable encounter together (see also Acts 22 and 26), it is quite clear that the light Paul saw was a real, visible, external light, for his companions saw it as well as he did. Indeed, they heard the voice too, though it seems they could not distinguish the words that were being spoken. Paul is very clear about this in his later writings. 'This was no waking dream,' he insists. 'It was a physical manifestation of the glorified body of the risen Christ' (see 1 Corinthians 15).

For him that was important, because although he was not numbered among the original twelve disciples who had followed Jesus during his days on earth, he was destined to become, like them, an apostle. And apostles were those who gained their understanding of the Christian gospel directly from the Master, and who could provide first-hand testimony to the historicity of the resurrection. Paul's claim to apostleship depended on the fact that he had 'seen' the Lord (1 Cor 9:1). So what we have here is not just the story of a conversion, but also of a calling to the special office of apostleship. And that is why the event was as supernatural as it was.

If you and I speak of 'seeing the light' as sometimes people do, it is in a much less literal sense than Paul does here, and we do not have to feel embarrassed about that for we are not apostles. Nevertheless, there are features of this experience which are characteristic of all conversions, and it is those which I want to identify particularly.

1. A divine initiative

First, conversion always involves a divine initiative. Paul was not consciously looking for this experience. Quite the reverse. So anxious was he to get to Damascus in order to expedite his programme of anti-Christian repression, he was still journeying in the heat of the midday sun when wiser Eastern travellers would have taken a break for the afternoon. Paul did not then decide he was going to get himself converted. Christ burst into his life and converted him. As he would testify again in one of his later letters, '[God] was pleased to reveal his Son in me' (Gal 1:15–16).

It is always like that. No true conversion ever takes

place in the context of self-congratulation. Conversion is an act of divine illumination as sovereign and as unilateral as that of creation itself. As Paul puts it, 'God, who said, "Let light shine out of darkness," made his light shine in our hearts to give us the light of the knowledge of the glory of God in the face of Christ' (2 Cor 4:6).

2. A personal encounter

Saul, Saul (9:4).

Notice the way Christ speaks to him by name. This is no detached academic debate Paul is engaging in, but a one-to-one conversation between him and Jesus. He knew a lot *about* Jesus already, but here for the first time a relationship has begun between them. These two persons have met and have started talking to one another. Conversion is never just the acceptance of a set of theological propositions. It goes far beyond the merely cerebral. It involves communicating with Jesus face to face. To put it simply, it means beginning to pray, and that in a most intimate and direct way.

3. A spiritual surrender

Who are you, Lord? (9:5).

It is true the title 'Lord' does not necessarily indicate divinity, but in the context of this extraordinary supernatural experience, it is quite impossible to think that Paul is using it as a mere formal politeness. No, this word 'Lord' is spoken in a tone of reverence and awe. Who was this extraordinary apparition? An archangel or the ghost of one of the prophets? Paul senses the answer to his own question, even as he is asking it. This is he whom Moses saw on Sinai; this is he whom Isaiah saw in the temple. This is not Gabriel or Elijah. This is the Lord! But now, to Paul's consternation, he has a new and unexpected name: 'I *am* Jesus, whom you are persecuting' (9:5).

There can be no conversion which does not issue in such a momentous recognition. A Christian convert is not one who merely believes Jesus was an historical person or a great spiritual leader, for Hindus and Muslims do that. A Christian is a person who acknowledges Jesus as 'the Lord'. No other title is adequate. In conversion, we are not merely paying our compliments to Jesus; we are offering him our lives.

Perhaps somebody reading this is wondering if they are converted. If so, you should not be misled by the special details of Paul's Damascus Road experience. There may not be any supernatural fireworks, or lightening-bolt from heaven for you. I cannot promise spiritual raptures or mystical ecstasies.

I can say with assurance, however, that if you are converted it will be because God has stepped into your life in a way you do not deserve, and possibly did not even seek. You may even, like Paul, be deliberately putting up barriers to his invasion. If you are converted, it will be as a result of his divine initiative.

If you are converted, it will be because Christ has spoken personally to your heart and you have personally responded to his word. It will not be because your family are Christians, or your friends are Christians, for there is no such thing as proxy repentance, or second-hand faith. It will be because, in the privacy of your own experience with God, he has called you by name, as he did Saul, and you have replied. In the moment of that exchange, every other person pales into insignificance. It is just Jesus and you.

And if you are converted, it will be because you have surrendered to Jesus as your Lord. I don't use the phrases 'decided for Christ' or 'committed to Christ', though decision and commitment are certainly involved. But conversion is at root not a decision, nor a commitment, but a *surrender* to the supreme authority of Jesus. A surrender that goes beyond mere verbal profession, and which expresses itself in the transformation of life and thought.

The person he became

> 'Now get up and go into the city, and you will be told what you must do.'
> The men travelling with Saul stood there speechless; they heard the sound but did not see anyone. Saul got up from the ground, but when he opened his eyes he could see nothing. So they led him by the hand into Damascus. For three days he was blind, and did not eat or drink anything (9:6–9).

Conversion then is not always accompanied by immediate floods of joy. For Paul, it was a profoundly humbling experience. That searching question the heavenly vision had asked went on haunting him for days. 'Why do you persecute me?' Paul could have replied, 'But I am not persecuting you, Master. I am persecuting these Christians.' But as Paul reflected on his experience, he realised to his shock that the two crimes were synonymous. It was no coincidence that he had seen a similarity between the death of Stephen and the crucifixion of Stephen's Master. The risen Christ was indeed inside these followers of his. As Paul would later explain in a startling metaphor to the believers at Corinth: 'You are the body of Christ' (1 Cor 12:27). The Spirit of Christ had incarnated himself afresh in his followers so whoever injured the church, therefore injured him.

The horror of the appalling sacrilege of which he had been guilty never left Paul. Years later he still spoke of himself as 'the least of the apostles...because I persecuted the church' (1 Cor 15:9). Broken-hearted at his folly he waited amid prayer and fasting in Damascus, unsure whether the blindness that had struck him was to be a permanent judgement from God against his sin, or whether perhaps there was some more hopeful purpose in this extraordinary revelation he had received. It is significant that the resolution to that uncertainty was provided not by another heavenly vision, but by a Christian pastor, a representative of that suffering body of Christ he had so viciously been persecuting.

In Damascus there was a disciple named Ananias. The Lord called to him in a vision, 'Ananias!'
'Yes, Lord,' he answered.
The Lord told him, 'Go to the house of Judas on Straight Street and ask for a man from Tarsus named Saul, for he is praying. In a vision he has seen a man named Ananias come and place his hands on him to restore his sight' (9:10–12).

It was a tragic irony, of course, that this arrogant young rabbi who came to Damascus to seek out the Christians should be reduced to a pathetic invalid who must himself be sought out by them. But seek him out they did, though not without understandable trepidation at the prospect.

> 'Lord,' Ananias answered, 'I have heard many reports about this man and all the harm he has done to your saints in Jerusalem. And he has come here with authority from the chief priests to arrest all who call on your name.'
> But the Lord said to Ananias, 'Go! This man is my chosen instrument to carry my name before the Gentiles and their kings and before the people of Israel. I will show him how much he must suffer for my name.'
> Then Ananias went to the house and entered it. Placing his hands on Saul, he said, 'Brother Saul' (9:13–17).

There is something extraordinarily moving about that. John Stott comments, 'These are the first words from Christian lips that Saul has heard since his conversion, and they are words of family affection.' Is there any other religion on earth that could move a person to display such courageous love to one he knew only as a callous enemy? That is surely what the church must always be doing. For if in persecuting the church Saul was persecuting Christ, then in being reconciled to Christ, he must also be reconciled to the church. The church is not permitted to hold grudges, for Christ does not.

How many broken-hearted souls are there in this world languishing in contrition for their sin, longing for some assurance of forgiveness, yearning for the Christian community to open its arms and welcome them into its family with words of such brotherly love, but who do not hear them? Perhaps if our ears were as open as Ananias' were to the voice of Christ, and if our hearts were moved by such a courageous love as his, then we would find ourselves being used by Christ more often to turn outsiders into insiders; enemies into friends; implacable persecutors of the church into its indomitable missionaries.

'Brother Saul, the Lord—Jesus, who appeared to you on the road as you were coming here—has sent me so that you may see again and be filled with the Holy Spirit.' Immediately, something like scales fell from Saul's eyes and he could see again. He got up and was baptised (9:17–18).

So the conversion is complete and sealed as it always is in the waters of repentance and renewal. Of course, it was not his baptism that converted him, any more than it was that supernatural vision that converted him. We know that the man who arose through those waters of baptism was a converted man because he was a changed man. Where there was once intolerant pride, now there would be chastened humility. Where once there was smug pharisaical self-righteousness, now there would be a consuming desire to know only Christ and the righteousness that comes by faith in him. Where once there was moral impotence and spiritual frigidity, there would be the power and the joy of the Holy Spirit. Where once there was fanatical ambition to destroy the churches, from now on there would be a consuming desire to multiply churches.

'This man is my chosen instrument to carry my name before the Gentiles' (9:15). So Christ had told Ananias and so it proved. Paul did more for the missionary expansion of the early church than all the rest of the apostles put together. With his conversion those ever-increasing circles of Christian influence were suddenly injected with a whole new wave of energy. Within days of his baptism we receive a foretaste of what is to come as he preaches in the Damascus synagogues that Jesus is the Son of God with such intellectual power and fiery conviction they could hardly believe it was the same man: 'Isn't he the man who caused havoc in Jerusalem among those who call on this name?' (9:21).

In a very real sense the old Saul of Tarsus was no more. 'If anyone is in Christ, he is a new creation; the old has gone, the new has come!' (2 Cor 5:17).

Are you converted?

Perhaps you have doubts. You cannot feel sure Jesus is really alive and you tremble at the risk Christianity represents. I can sympathise with such hesitation. Conversion is bound to feel risky—like getting married, you can't be completely sure of the ground before you step out into it. It feels like a gamble—a step of faith into vulnerability and insecurity. But sometimes it's only by taking such risks that we discover the best that life can offer us. And consider, is it not a most remarkable proof of the resurrection of Jesus Christ that this man, Paul of all people, should be converted? After all, he was there on the spot in Jerusalem. No one had more opportunity to investigate the truth of the claims of Christianity, nor more motivation to do so. If that tomb had not been empty, and if the reports of what happened on that first Easter Sunday were not credible, Paul would most certainly have known. He had more reason than anybody to prove that the Christians were liars and charlatans. And yet, as he rode out on that Damascus Road, he did so not as a man secure in the knowledge that Christianity was an indefensible nonsense, but as a man plagued with inner anxiety that it might very well be the truth. If a first-century man as prejudiced against Christianity as Paul could be converted, is it then such intellectual suicide for you to think you might be converted?

Or perhaps your problem is not doubt but unworthiness. You feel that you do not deserve to be a Christian. You do not belong in the company of high-minded, morally respectable church-goers. You think of all those secret sins which we are all at pains to conceal, even from our closest friends, and feel that you are not good enough.

Have you not realised yet that goodness has nothing to do with it? This man Saul of Tarsus wanted the Christians dead. If he had personally driven the nails through the hands of the crucified Christ, he could not have been more viciously antagonistic in his cause. Yet Christ appeared to him, forgave him, restored him and converted him. 'Here is a trustworthy saying,' Paul would say later to his friend Timothy. 'Christ Jesus came into the world to save sinners—of whom I am the worst' (1 Tim 1:15). If he can save the worst of sinners, can he not save you? Of course you feel unworthy, but you must believe me when I say that the love and grace of Christ is greater than your record of failure and weakness.

I am reminded of John Masefield's great poem, 'The Everlasting Mercy', in which he recounts the story of another Saul: Saul Kane, an inebriated boxer, who during a night of alcoholic excess encounters a courageous young Quaker woman. She enters the pub where he is getting drunk, to witness to Christ.

She up to me with black eyes wide,
She looked as though her spirit cried;
She took my tumbler from the bar
Beside where all the matches are
And poured it out upon the floor-dust,
among the fag ends, spit and sawdust.
'Saul Kane,' she said, 'when next you drink,
Do me the gentleness to think
That every drop of drink accursed
Makes Christ within you die of thirst,
That every dirty word you say
is one more flint upon His way,
Another thorn about His head
Another mock by where He tread,
Another nail, another cross.
All that you are is that Christ's loss.'

Suddenly, the poem says, like that other Saul on the Damascus Road, Saul Kane is smitten to the heart by the conviction of his sin.

Headlong he rushes from the pub, first in an agony of shame, and then as he sobers up trudging along the country lanes, a glorious emancipation begins to fill his heart.

I did not think, I did not strive
The deep peace burnt my me alive;
The bolted door had broken in,
I knew that I had done with sin
I knew that Christ had given me birth
To brother all the souls on earth,
And every bird and every beast
Should share the crumbs broke at the feast.

O glory of the lighted mind
How dead I'd been, how dumb, how blind,
The station brook to my new eyes

Was babbling out of Paradise;
The waters rushing from the rain
Were singing Christ has risen again.
I thought all earthly creatures knelt
From rapture of the joy I felt.

Are you converted? I do not ask, 'Have you seen the heavenly light as Saul of Tarsus did?' I do not even ask, 'Have you felt the ecstatic euphoria of Saul Kane in that poem?' The test is not, 'Has something supernatural happened around you?' but, 'Has something supernatural happened within you?' Whatever you were in the past, are you able to confess: 'Jesus Christ is Lord of my life,' and mean it? Because if you can, I give you God's word that you are converted. However unspectacular your spiritual experience may seem by comparison to the Damascus Road, you have passed from death to life. Like Paul you ought to be baptised and identify with the Christian community. There are many Ananiases who are longing to call you their brother or their sister.

If, however, you cannot confess Jesus Christ as your Lord, then I must tell you solemnly that no matter how lurid the testimonies may be of your spiritual experiences in the past, you are not converted. You may be on your Damascus Road, but you have not yet had dealings with the risen Christ. Could it be that even now, as you consider the conversion of the apostle, you hear Christ's voice addressing you personally by name, just as he did? Could it be that even at this moment heaven is waiting with bated breath to hear you respond, 'Lord'?

8

Overcoming Prejudice in the Church

Acts 10:11–18

'Surely not, Lord!' Peter replied. 'I have never eaten anything impure or unclean.' The voice spoke to him a second time, 'Do not call anything impure that God has made clean.'

Acts 10:14–15

THIS WORLD is not made up just of many people, but of many peoples. There are thousands of human groups; some based on different languages, some on different religions. Some derive from social class or from ethnic origin, some require the members of their group to be of a certain age, or of a certain sex or even require their members to share the same taste in pop music or fashion. One thing, however, that every human group has in common is a culture which enables it to define its distinctives and to protect its identity.

The vast majority of the social and political divisions that trouble our world today find their roots in the cultural prejudice that keeps such groups apart. In South Africa it is black and white. In Sri Lanka it is Tamil and Singhalese. In Northern Ireland it is Catholic and Protestant. In North India it is Muslim and Hindu. And in Europe it often seems to be Britain versus the rest. Ironically, the nationalism we fear so much in our European neighbours is just as conspicuous among the British. These small islands boast at least four nationalisms: English, Scottish, Welsh and Irish—not counting the local chauvinisms you find in places like Cornwall or Yorkshire.

147

We pointed out in chapter 1 that such human groups cannot be easily assimilated or integrated, for culture is an extraordinarily resilient social force which survives in the face of the most deliberate attempts to suppress it. Events in Eastern Europe and in Soviet Russia in the early 1990s illustrate very dramatically that forgotten peoples who have been denied self-determination for the best part of a century can suddenly re-emerge and assert their independence. Empires do not last, no matter how benevolent their paternalism or how cruel their oppression; at the end of the day, they always fall. It is cultures that survive. Empires are held together only by military or bureaucratic organisation, but culture is organically embedded in the very social psychology of a people. I do not think there is any political utopianism so surely doomed to disillusionment as that which seeks to make the divided peoples of this world one, simply by drawing lines on a map.

According to the Book of Revelation, it is not until the coming of Christ in glory that the balm will become available to reverse the ancient curse of Babel. The leaves of the tree of life which are in the midst of New Jerusalem, are 'for the healing of the nations' (Rev 22:2). Until the arrival of that heavenly remedy, wisdom declares that we construct political solutions that preserve group identities, for the imperialism that seeks arbitrarily to unite those whom culture divides, is doomed to failure, and far from contributing to world peace, it is simply an invitation to war.

However, even if cultural prejudice cannot be dissolved by international diplomacy, it is the intention of the Book of Acts to show us one society in which its divisive poison is neutralised. It is almost as if one of the leaves of that supernatural tree in the New Jerusalem had floated down from heaven prematurely, and touched the earth to start healing national wounds here and now. Indeed, in a very real sense that is what is happening. The Holy Spirit is the power of the age to come. He generates in Christian communities a glimpse of that future world when the nations will beat their swords into ploughshares. And nowhere is his miraculous activity in this regard more obvious than when he overcomes prejudice in the church.

'I now realise how true it is that God does not show favouritism but accepts men from every nation who fear him and do what is right' (10:34–35). It is quite impossible to exaggerate the mind-blowing revolution such a sentiment represented in the first-century world. Peter was a Palestinian Jew, and in the entire history of the world there has never been a more xenophobic group. The rabbis had interpreted the covenant with Abraham in such an exclusive way that any contact at all with a non-Jew was a sin: it was forbidden even to help a Gentile mother in childbirth because to do so would simply bring another pagan into the world. In the words of one rabbinical proverb, the Gentiles were created by God simply as fuel for the flames of hell. That was the climate in which this man Peter had been raised.

More remarkable still, the man to whom he is speaking these words is a Roman soldier. There was no group of Gentiles more obnoxious to first-century Palestinian Jews, for the Roman army was an oppressive instrument of colonial occupation in Israel. Many of Peter's Galilean countrymen had been slaughtered by Roman legionnaires in reprisals for patriotic uprisings and attempted *coups d'etat*. The Jews did not just hold Romans in contempt because they were pagans, they loathed and despised them as mortal enemies. Yet here we have a first-century Palestinian Jew saying to a Gentile Roman soldier, 'I now realise how true it is that God does not show favouritism but accepts men from every nation that fear him and do what is right.' It is almost an understatement to call it a miracle. However did Peter change from being a man full of prejudice to an evangelist who was able to win Roman soldiers for Christ? Luke's narrative suggests there were three factors involved, and they may well hold the clue to how we too may overcome prejudice in our church.

Experience of foreign travel

As Peter travelled about the country, he went to visit the saints in Lydda (9:32).

Now of course this was not the first time that Peter had conducted this kind of itinerant ministry. When he had been with Jesus, he had travelled around Palestine quite extensively. But since his Master's death and resurrection, Peter and the other apostles had led a much more sedentary life. They had had their hands full, building up the rapidly growing congregation in Jerusalem. And even when persecution broke out after the martyrdom of Stephen, they stayed on in Jerusalem rather than seeking refuge with the rest of the Christians in the comparative safety of more distant provinces.

The impetus then for Peter to leave Jerusalem had not come from any particular desire to travel. The need had been forced upon him as a result of Philip's missionary enterprise which we were looking at in chapter 6. We noted there how Philip had gone up to Samaria, and without any authorisation from the church's leadership preached the gospel to non-Jews. He did so with great success, the Samaritan population responding by the hundred. So Peter and his colleague John had travelled up to Samaria to find out what was going on and to regularise the situation. It had been, no doubt, a thrilling experience for them to see the power of the Holy Spirit transforming Samaritan lives. But it must have made Peter think as well, for if God was willing to convert Samaritans to Christ, where was the expansion of Christian testimony going to end? He probably knew nothing of Philip's later encounter with the Ethiopian, or of Paul's conversion and very special vocation to Gentile mission. But such questions must nevertheless have been brooding in his mind. Perhaps that is why he decided to extend his leave of absence from Jerusalem in order to visit other groups of Christians who had been scattered by the persecution, to see what sort of response they were receiving in their new locations. Luke mentions two particular places which were on his itinerary: Lydda and Joppa. His interest in these towns is due in part to the fact that in each of them Peter performed notable miracles. At Lydda a paralytic was enabled to walk, and at Joppa a woman named Dorcas was raised from the dead. Both these signs are recorded in such a way that they are reminiscent of similar miracles performed by Jesus, for Luke wants us to realise that the risen Jesus is still at work—just as he said in the very opening words of his book.

Luke, however, also makes two significant observations about Peter's ministry in those towns: 'All those who lived in Lydda and Sharon saw him and turned to the Lord' (9:35). 'This became known all over Joppa, and many people believed in the Lord' (9:42).

Lydda and Joppa were towns of western Palestine, territory which had once belonged to the Philistines and which, even in the first century, was still decidedly semi-pagan. The wide degree of spiritual responsiveness that Peter witnessed in these towns must indicate that there was a profound impact not only on the Jews but also on non-Jews who lived in the area. It may be significant that Philip recently conducted a preaching tour in this region on his way up the coast from Gaza to Caesarea. Perhaps Peter was once again following in the footsteps of that adventurous young evangelist—this time fresh from his encounter with the Ethiopian eunuch.

Certainly there is a hint that Peter's Judaistic strait-jacket was being loosened a little by this experience of foreign travel. For we read: 'Peter stayed in Joppa for some time with a tanner named Simon' (9:43). Tanning was regarded by strict Jews as an unclean occupation because it involved handling animals that were not kosher. Peter's willingness to accept hospitality in a home so saturated with an atmosphere of ceremonial defilement must surely indicate that his Jewish scruples were being moderated. There can be no question that God was using Peter's experiences, first in Samaria and now in the coastal plain of Western Palestine, to make him question his Jewish prejudices. In fact this passage illustrates a vital factor in overcoming prejudice in anybody's life. If Peter had stayed in Jerusalem, I do not believe we would have ever heard him say, 'I realise now that God does not show favouritism.' It was partly, at least, as a result of his personal exposure to other cultures and their response to Christianity that he began to see the foolishness of discriminatory attitudes. And it may very well be the same for us.

Nothing has contributed more to the shattering of my English insularity than the decision my wife and I took to live in Africa for a few years. It is only by getting outside your own country that you begin to view its culture objectively; to see its strengths and weaknesses. Indeed, there are certain troublespots, like Northern Ireland for instance, where I am persuaded sectarianism would be moderated in a matter of weeks if every member of the divided community were given a return air ticket to some other part of the world. Parochialism feeds prejudice; and there is nothing like foreign travel to break it down. Go and live somewhere else for a month or two, try to learn a different language, and share in a different culture, and you will come back as Peter did: different. You will find perhaps, without even being fully conscious of it, that you are making your church different too.

Spiritual insight

About noon the following day as they were approaching the city, Peter went up on the roof to pray. He became hungry and wanted something to eat, and while the meal was being prepared, he fell into a trance. He saw heaven opened and something like a large sheet being let down to earth by its four corners. It contained all kinds of four-footed animals, as well as reptiles of the earth and birds of the air. Then a voice told him, 'Get up, Peter. Kill and eat' (10:9–13).

Now, although this experience is later called a vision, I think it is significant to note that it was not a direct, unambiguous divine revelation. It was cryptic and puzzling. Peter was left 'wondering about the meaning of the vision' (10:17), for it took as its subject not racial prejudice but the much narrower issue of Jewish food regulations. It is well known that Jews do not eat pork, but that is only one of a vast range of dietary prohibitions which are laid down in the Old Testament law. Pious Jews of the first century believed that by observing these rules they witnessed to their special privilege as the chosen race. But I suspect that Peter was already beginning to question these ancient taboos about what he could and could not eat. After all, Jesus had shown scant respect for such Jewish ceremonial regulations on occasions: 'Nothing that enters a man from the outside can make him "unclean" ' (Mk 7:19).

Consider also the people he had been mixing with on his journeyings, many of whom were either not Jews at all or very bad Jews from the point of view of ceremonial holiness. They did not observe the kosher food regulations and yet were responding to the gospel in a marvellous way. Simon the tanner, a Christian believer, was giving him generous hospitality just because he was a brother in Christ. 'But if I were to keep the rules strictly,' Peter must have thought to himself, 'I would not be able to share his table or even shake his hand because he has been touching pig skins all day.'

Such radical and disturbing thoughts might have been buzzing in Peter's mind as a result of his experiences. Imagine him, then, kneeling to pray on that flat roof of Simon's house, as he did every day at noon, and finding himself in the midst of his meditations hungry and sleepy in the midday heat. Up the stairs perhaps is wafting the aroma of Simon's wife's cooking pot with lunch on the boil, and from the ground below the parapet there comes the less congenial stench of Simon's animal skins stretched out in the sun. Maybe out at sea he can see the sail of a ship blowing in the wind. It is not hard to envisage how God might have woven together this mix of stimuli and ideas in Peter's subconscious to produce the rather strange dream he saw, and used it to crystalise the spiritual insights which Peter had been coming to for a long while: 'Then a voice told him, "Get up, Peter. Kill and eat." "Surely not, Lord!" Peter replied. "I have never eaten anything impure or unclean." The voice spoke to him a second time, "Do not call anything impure that God has made clean" ' (10:13–15).

At that moment there occurred what appeared to be a coincidence but which, as Peter later discovered, was in fact a divinely engineered synchronisation. For at the precise moment that he was pondering the meaning of the vision: 'Men sent by Cornelius found out where Simon's house was and stopped at the gate. They called out, asking if Simon who was known as Peter was staying there' (10:17–18).

If Peter was in any doubt about the divine providence that was ordering his experience it was dispelled by the unmistakable pressure of the Holy Spirit in his heart. 'You must run with this ball, Peter. Do not be frightened of the consequences.'

'So get up and go downstairs. Do not hesitate to go with them, for I have sent them' (10:20). Interestingly, you could equally well translate the Greek word translated 'hesitate' as 'discriminate'. 'Don't discriminate against them, Peter, in spite of the fact that they are Gentiles.' Even a mind as inured in cultural prejudice as Peter's was could not fail to work out the implication. The vision may have overtly challenged only his ideas of unclean food, but he could see that its real significance was far more revolutionary than that. And when he arrived at Cornelius' house he told them so: 'You are well aware that it is against our law for a Jew to associate with a Gentile or visit him. But God has shown me that I should not call any man impure or unclean. So when I was sent for, I came without raising any objection' (10:28–29).

Here then, quite clearly, is the second factor in the breakdown of Peter's ethnocentricity: a spiritual insight into the mind of God on the matter. His religion was astray, in spite of all its biblical orthodoxy, for it had led him to believe that God was prejudiced against Gentiles when, in fact, he was nothing of the kind. Sadly that is one theological discovery that many Christians still need to make. Over the years Christianity has sometimes been used, just as Judaism was used in the first century, to support discriminatory practices and attitudes. The Bible has been quoted in the defence of slavery in the southern states of the USA, and to legitimise apartheid in South Africa. It has been exploited to endorse class discrimination in Victorian England and anti-Semitism in Nazi Germany. The degree of moral blindness to which professing Christians have sometimes been led in this area is quite appalling, and we must beware lest unwittingly we are still subject to that same defect in our vision.

What would be in that sheet let down from heaven if God were to give us a vision such as he gave Peter to disperse our prejudices? For some of us, perhaps, an electric guitar would be included because our chief prejudice is against the culture of youth; for others an academic gown might well be in the sheet, because our chief prejudice is against intellectuals; for some a video of *Eastenders*, maybe, because our chief prejudice is against the working classes; and for still others a Tandoori chicken because our chief prejudice is against immigrants. All sorts of things might be found in our sheet from heaven because spiritual insight into the fallaciousness of our prejudices is something we all need. God sees this world in glorious technicolor, a tapestry of races, tribes and groups who are all made in his divine image. He rejoices in every one of them without exception, and they all need Christ the Saviour of the world. Only when we begin to see the world as he does will prejudice be eliminated in our churches.

Experience of cross cultural evangelism

[Peter said,] 'May I ask why you sent for me?'
Cornelius answered, 'Four days ago I was in my house praying at this hour, at three in the afternoon. Suddenly a man in shining clothes stood before me and said, "Cornelius, God has heard your prayer and remembered your gifts to the poor. Send to Joppa for Simon who is called Peter. He is a guest in the home of Simon the tanner, who lives by the sea." So I sent for you immediately, and it was good of you to come. Now we are all here in the presence of God to listen to everything the Lord has commanded you to tell us' (10:29–33).

There could scarcely be a more favourable opportunity for preaching the gospel than that! Here is a man who is already a pious, conscientious worshipper of God and who has been instructed by angels in advance to invite the evangelist to his house. Here is a man who holds that evangelist in such esteem that he falls at his feet when he comes to the door, and has solemnly gathered his entire household together in keen anticipation of hearing a vitally important word from God through him. There was only one thing that could possibly deter Peter from discharging his duty as a preacher in such circumstances, and in earlier days that deterrent might very well have been enough. Cornelius was a Gentile, he had never been circumcised and did not belong to the covenant people of God. According to the rules of his religious upbringing, Peter should not even have been under the same roof with such a man, But Peter has learned a lot in the weeks since Pentecost. 'I now realise how true it is that God does not show favouritism but accepts men from every nation who fear him and do what is right' (10:34–35).

Peter is not saying here that all morally respectable people go to heaven. If that were true Peter would not have had to instruct Cornelius later on his need for the forgiveness of sins. Neither is Peter saying here that all religions lead to God, although some commentators have interpreted these words in that way. If that were so he would not have had to instruct Cornelius about the unique office of Jesus as the Judge of all mankind: 'He had commanded us to preach to the people and to testify that he is the one whom God appointed as judge of the living and the dead. All the prophets testify about him' (10:42–43).

No, there is no universalism here encouraging the thought that pious pagans get to heaven without Christ. What Peter is saying when he speaks of God not showing favouritism is that, while he had believed once that God was a racialist, he realises now that the marks of God's grace can be seen just as readily in Gentile lives as they can in Jewish lives. For those marks are not cultural, but moral and spiritual. As Paul puts it in his great letter to the Romans: 'A man is not a Jew if he is only one outwardly...a man is a Jew if he is one inwardly' (Rom 2:28–29).

If there were any lingering doubts troubling Peter's heart regarding this controversial step that he had taken in offering the messianic kingdom to Gentiles, God once again silences those doubts in an absolutely unmistakable fashion: 'While Peter was still speaking these words, the Holy Spirit came on all who heard the message. The circumcised believers who had come with Peter were astonished that the gift of the Holy Spirit had been poured out even on the Gentiles. For they heard them speaking in tongues and praising God' (10:44–46).

It was just like Pentecost all over again! Only this time it was Gentile tongues that were filled with supernatural ecstasy. There could be no question then that it was God's intention to include Cornelius and his household in the church of Jesus Christ, and if that was so, why should there be any further delay in placing upon them the mark of family membership? ' "Can anyone keep these people from being baptised with water? They have received the Holy Spirit just as we have." So he ordered that they be baptised in the name of Jesus Christ' (10:47–48).

This was an absolutely crucial moment in the life of the early church. It is true Cornelius may not have been strictly the first Gentile convert—the Ethiopian eunuch had been that. But now a leading apostle had placed his imprimatur on Gentile conversion, and within days the news was spreading like wildfire!

Predictably of course Peter got hauled over the coals for what he had done: 'The Apostles and the brothers throughout Judea heard that the Gentiles also had received the word of God. So when Peter went up to Jerusalem, the circumcised believers criticised him and said, "You went into the house of uncircumcised men and ate with them" ' (11:1–3).

Church leaders who try to break down walls of prejudice will often find that they have to face objections from less open-minded representatives of their own constituency. But Peter's defence is quite unanswerable. Patiently he reports to these Jewish conservatives in Jerusalem everything that had happened to him—the chain of events that had led inevitably to his decision to baptise Cornelius—including the visit to foreign parts that had opened his mind, the spiritual insight he had gained from his dream, the extraordinary coincidence of Cornelius' delegates arriving at precisely that moment, the inner assurance of the Holy Spirit that encouraged him not to let his Jewish scruples deter him, the remarkable state of spiritual preparedness in which he had found Cornelius (converted almost before he had even uttered a word) and of course that final pentecostal confirmation:

As I began to speak, the Holy Spirit came on them as he had come on us at the beginning. Then I remembered what the Lord had said, 'John baptised with water, but you will be baptised with the Holy Spirit.' So if God gave them the same gift as he gave us, who believed in the Lord Jesus Christ, who am I to think that I could oppose God! (11:15–17).

One senses that Luke has an amused tongue in his

cheek as he records the astonished conclusion of Peter's conservative Christian brothers: 'So then, God has even granted the Gentiles repentance unto life' (11:18).

Of course prejudice was not eliminated over night. Luke records later on in the Book of Acts that the issue of Gentile membership of the church exploded into a major controversy a few years later (see Acts 15). Culture is very resilient and cultural prejudice is therefore very difficult to overcome. But God had accomplished his immediate purpose. Philip was no longer a lonely eccentric. The appointed leadership of the apostolic church in Jerusalem was now committed to Gentile evangelisation and the way was clear for other congregations, less hampered by tradition and prejudice, to drive through the gate which Peter had opened.

But have we crossed its threshold completely? Politics in a fallen world has to accept the alienations of Babel, and is foolish if it does not. But the church of Jesus Christ, empowered by the Holy Spirit, must seek to overcome those alienations. The New Covenant community is to reflect heaven, not this fallen world, and because of that every form of discrimination and prejudice is out of place. Yet we have ethnic churches which make it quite clear that their membership is limited to people of a certain colour. We have class-bound churches which make it quite clear that only affluent middle-class members are welcomed through its doors, or indeed into its car park. We have churches for geriatrics, which do not expect anybody in their churches under the age of fifty-five, and we have churches for ravers, which make it quite clear that they do not expect anybody in their churches over the age of twenty-five. We have racist churches, tribalist churches and we have sexist churches too.

We must beware of a self-deceit in this matter too. It is possible to pretend we hold a very liberal and tolerant attitude, until a family from a culture other than our own moves in next door, or our daughter comes home and says she wants to marry someone from another race.

Christians cannot yield to prejudice, for they serve a God who does not show favouritism. He may have sent the good news to Israel first, but he intends it for everybody. There is no room then in New Testament Christianity for segregated congregations. Chauvinistic rivalries may well continue to divide the nations, but they must not be allowed to divide the Christian community.

9

The Church that Changed the World

Acts 11:19–30, 13:1–3

Some of them, however, men from Cyprus and Cyrene, went to Antioch and began speaking to the Greeks also, telling them the good news about the Lord Jesus. The Lord's hand was with them, and a great number of people believed and turned to the Lord.

Acts 11:20–21

I N 1990 there were about 5.1 billion people in the world of whom about 1.7 billion would call themselves Christians. Of course, not all who profess Christianity actually practise it. It is difficult to determine what proportion of that 1.7 billion we should regard as truly spiritually alive. But the best estimates available suggest a figure of something like 0.5 billion might be reasonable. That is 500 million committed Christians in a world of over 5,000 million people.

From one point of view that is quite an encouraging statistic. It means, for instance, that there are five times as many committed Christians in the world today as constituted the entire population of the world in the day of St Paul. It means there is one committed Christian for every nine uncommitted or unconverted people, as compared with one for every 200 as there was at the end of the first century AD. In fact the ratio of Christian to non-Christian has been steadily improving for the last 200 years.

There is another less optimistic side to the story, however. Of the 4.6 billion in this world who are not committed Christians, over a quarter (1.3 billion) are still 'unreached'. By that I do not mean that they would not call themselves Christian. I mean that they have no meaningful opportunity to discover what a Christian is, because there are no churches in the orbit of their social existence that might tell them about Jesus Christ. Many of the 1.3 billion 'unreached' lie behind high walls of cultural prejudice, and even ideological antagonism to Christianity. They include 650 completely unreached people groups and eighty mega cities, some of them with populations larger than London. And many of these people live in one of the countries which have closed their borders to conventional missionary activity. The line then between 3.8 billion in the world who are within range of the local evangelism of Christian churches, and the 1.3 billion who lie beyond that range, represents for us in the 1990s the boundary of Christian influence.

Those ever-increasing circles of testimony by which Jesus predicted his disciples would penetrate the world with the gospel are still expanding even today, 2,000 years later. First in Jerusalem, then in Judea and Samaria, and then to the ends of the earth, he said. And the line between the 'reached and 'unreached' marks the edge of that expanding wave front. There is no way the 1.3 billion 'unreached' can be incorporated into the 'reached' peoples of the world, except as the result of missionary endeavour. They represent the church's unfinished evangelistic task. Adventurous Christians must leave the emotional security and the physical safety of their own society and deliberately seek to plant churches and win converts in those cultures where as yet there are few, or none.

In our final study in the Book of Acts we find the early Christians facing precisely the same challenge.

It presents to us the birth of missionary vision in the churches; or to be more accurate, the birth of missionary vision in *a church*, because according to Luke the first pioneering step towards planned cross-cultural mission was taken by a single congregation, the church at Antioch. It rightly deserves to be called the church that changed the world. In this chapter we shall discover the source of their vision and try to identify the factors which inspired their missionary activity.

Grass-roots evangelistic zeal

Now those who had been scattered by the persecution in connection with Stephen travelled as far as Phoenicia, Cyprus and Antioch, telling the message only to Jews. Some of them, however, men from Cyprus and Cyrene, went to Antioch and began to speak to Greeks also, telling them the good news about the Lord Jesus. The Lord's hand was with them and a great number of people believed and turned to the Lord (11:19–21).

We have seen in previous chapters how the hostility of the Jewish authorities, following the martyrdom of Stephen, had led to a dispersion of the young church in Jerusalem. First Philip, and then Peter, carried the seed of the Christian message into new soil as a result of this centrifugal movement. Now Luke highlights yet another zone of expansion. Some of those persecuted believers went even further afield, to Antioch, the capital of the Roman province of Syria and the third largest city in the world at that time. Unlike Jerusalem it was a cosmopolitan secularised city. Though it had a sizable Jewish community, it was predominantly pagan and had a notorious reputation for sexual immorality as a result of some of the Greek and Asian religious cults that thrived there. In a pluralist urban environment like that, it was very difficult for a preacher to limit his target audience, even if he wanted to, and some of these young Christian émigrés to the city refused even to try. In their enthusiasm for their new-found Christian faith they shared the gospel, Luke tells us, not only with their fellow Jews but with Gentiles also. It may be significant that Luke uses a slightly unusual word to describe these non-Jewish contacts; not 'Greeks' as our translation renders it, but 'Hellenists'. That is a title which has aroused some scholarly debate, but it probably implies that, like Cornelius, these folk were people who, though of Greek culture, were nevertheless very sympathetic to Judaism. There were many such people in the ancient world, and in a liberal place like Antioch, some of them may well have attended the synagogue regularly and would have met these newly-arrived Christian refugees from Jerusalem there. Luke does not tell us the names of the Jewish Christians who defied the kosher taboo and spoke to these Gentiles. But he does tell us they were of Cypriot and Cyrenean origin, and again that is probably significant. It means that, unlike the conservative Palestinian Jews who had grown up in the cloistered Hebraic culture of Judea, these were men and women of the world. They spoke Greek, not Aramaic, as their preferred language, and did not feel the same degree of instinctive anti-Gentile prejudice as, for instance, Peter would have done. For that reason, they did not need a divine vision to persuade them it was acceptable to preach to Gentiles. Almost certainly, as businessmen in the Roman Empire, they would have had to talk to Gentiles all the time, whatever the Jerusalem rabbis thought about it.

I suspect, however, that even they must have been slightly taken aback by the scale of the response which their witness to these Gentiles produced: 'The Lord's hand was with them and a great number of people believed and turned to the Lord' (11:21).

There are two things which are worth noting about this prolific spiritual responsiveness in relationship to the missionary task that faces us today. First, it highlights the *strategic importance of big cities* in Christian mission. Breaking through cultural barriers with the gospel is invariably easier in an urban setting like Antioch, because people who live in big cities are already less attached to their traditional roots than their contemporaries in rural communities are. The pluralism of the city invites more open-mindedness as it exposes people to different cultures and challenges their preconceived ideas. Its comparative anonymity also makes it much easier for people to contemplate changing their behaviour patterns in fundamental ways.

Of course, cities have their disadvantages. Morally and spiritually they can become very decadent. But as far as Christian mission is concerned, that does not stop them being places where the citadels of pagan culture and ideology are most vulnerable. The early Christians certainly found it so at Antioch, and the twentieth-century evangelist will find it so too. Without wishing to underestimate the importance of reaching out to rural areas, strategically speaking, the increasing urbanisation of our world today is an enormous advantage to the gospel. Many of the 1.3 billion 'unreached' live in vast anti-Christian cities

169

like Teheran, Kabul, Istanbul, Tashkent and Karachi, and many of that unconverted 2.1 billion who are already within reach of Christian mission are also located in great urban centres like Calcutta, Tokyo, Djakarta, Seoul, Bangkok and Havana. It is cities like these that are the Antiochs of our modern world and which hold the key to the completion of the missionary task.

Secondly, the response gained at Antioch highlights the *strategic importance of grass-roots evangelism*. You will notice how careful Luke is to stress the sovereign providence of God behind the growth of the church there. It was 'the Lord's hand' (11:21) that was primarily responsible for their success, multiplying the church at Antioch just as he had added to the church daily in Jerusalem. But that does not negate the fact that it was the personal witness of the Cypriot and Cyrenean Christians that he chose to use to accomplish his sovereign purpose. Cornelius, remember, had had an angelic vision, but the angel had not told him the good news of Jesus. God insisted that it had to be Peter who did that. So too here, though no doubt God could have found supernatural ways to turn these Gentiles to himself, he chose to use the testimony of Christians. That is his appointed means, and for that reason no church will ever become a missionary church unless it possesses a vigorous grass-roots concern for personal outreach to the non-Christian world where it is. If it is not concerned for local evangelism on the doorstep, it is not going to be concerned for cross-cultural mission a thousand miles away. Many churches in Britain try to be like lighthouses, illuminating distant lands, but leaving the area around their bases plunged in darkness. But real missionary vision cannot be generated in a congregation which is introverted and parochial. A primary requirement of mission is that there shall be a body of people in the church who are passionately committed to evangelism, as these men of Cyprus and Cyrene clearly were. Personal witness was part of their lifestyle; they did not organise witness teams, or get trained at Bible college before they felt qualified or motivated to witness to others. Like Philip, they demonstrated a spontaneous openness in sharing their faith.

Perhaps the fact that they were Hellenistic rather than Palestinian assisted in that. For it is often true that those who have grown up in a culture which is heavily influenced by the Bible find themselves handicapped in evangelism. The spark of evangelistic fire is almost always strongest in those who have grown up in a pagan environment and who feel at home in it. That is why many people believe that the greatest resource for Christian mission in the twenty-first century is not going to be found in the Christianised West any longer, but in the burgeoning young churches in Latin America, Africa and East Asia. These are the contemporary men of Cyprus and Cyrene who demonstrate the Christian commitment and enthusiasm for evangelism which is going to be necessary if the missionary task of the church us going to be completed.

An encouraging pastor

News of this reached the ears of the church at Jerusalem, and they sent Barnabas to Antioch. When he arrived and saw the evidence of the grace of God, he was glad and encouraged them all to remain true to the Lord with all their hearts. He was a good man, full of the Holy Spirit and faith, and a great number of people were brought to the Lord (11:22–24).

It is not difficult to imagine that the church at Antioch must have been very different from the one in Jerusalem. The number of converted Greeks may well have exceeded the number of Christian Jews there. So, for the first time, we have a congregation which is predominantly Gentile in origin. It is no wonder that the apostles in Jerusalem were concerned to ensure that there was no heretical sectarianism emerging as a result. In a similar situation following Philip's successful evangelism in Samaria, you will remember they sent the apostles Peter and John to investigate. It may be that as a result of Peter's experience in the conversion of Cornelius, the church in Jerusalem had become a little less paranoid about the church planting activities of its dispersed members now. For on this occasion they do not send two heavy-weight apostles, but one very gentle pastor. What a wise choice Barnabas turned out to be. His real name was Joseph, but the apostles called him Barnabas because it fitted his character so well; in Aramaic it means 'son of encouragement', and it was certainly in encouraging that he excelled.

'[He] saw the evidence of the grace of God' (11:23). We have to read that against the background of the fact that there were things going on in Antioch which many conservative Jewish Christians back in Jerusalem would have frowned upon most seriously. Almost certainly there was table fellowship between Jews and Gentiles; Gentiles were being accepted into the church without circumcision; very possibly there was a loosening up of the kosher food regulations in Jewish homes; it is likely that church services were being conducted in a way considerably less influenced by synagogue liturgy than would have been the case down in Jerusalem too. Perhaps husbands even sat next to their wives! In a cosmopolitan city like Antioch, this Gentile church would have inevitably had a more radical, experimental feel to it.

But we hear no 'ifs' and 'buts' from Barnabas' lips. He could easily have been a wet blanket, could he not? Indeed, had he been less wise and diplomatic, he could have generated a rift between Antioch and Jerusalem, as serious as that which later divided Constantinople and Rome. But: 'He was a good man, full of the Holy Spirit and faith...When he arrived and saw the evidence of the grace of God, he was glad' (11:23–24).

Here was a man of wide vision and generous heart. He observed lives changed from pagan immorality to Christian holiness and, circumcised or not, kosher or not, he recognised that this was the grace of God at work. 'He...encouraged them all to remain true to the Lord with all their hearts' (11:23).

What a fillip that must have been to this young and enthusiastic congregation; to have a man of such eminence pat them on the back and endorse their work. Little wonder we read that a great number of people were brought to the Lord. An encouraging pastor like this was an immense asset to the church's advance. He augmented the impact of the Christian community on its environment by his Christian example, and he inspired the evangelistic endeavour of the Cyrenian and Cypriot church members by his enthusiasm for what they were doing.

It is unlikely that any church will be a missionary church without pastoral gifts like that within it. Indeed, I have to say, if I am to be frank, that one of the reasons some of the most biblical and conservative churches are lacking missionary vision today is that their pastors remind me not so much of Barnabas, the Son of Encouragement, as of Caiaphas the High Priest. They are men of rigid and inflexible mind, so confined in their denominational traditionalism they judge anybody who does not conform to their stereotype of Christian spirituality as a heretic, or a worldling. Instead of fostering grass-roots initiative among their members, they feel threatened by it; instead of applauding the evidence of God's grace in enthusiastic young Christian lives, they are suspicious of it. Rather than enjoying new developments in worship, they are critical of them, and instead of encouraging new converts, they often turn them away by the austerity of their bearing.

We desperately need more pastors like Barnabas. Men who are more interested in authentic Christianity than the preservation of their own traditions, or the propagation of their particular denominational label: sons of encouragement, rather than bigots with fixed ideas.

A theological teacher

> Then Barnabas went to Tarsus to look for Saul, and when he found him, he brought him to Antioch. So for a whole year Barnabas and Saul met with the church and taught great numbers of people. The disciples were first called Christians at Antioch (11:25–26).

This is important, because it reminds us that all the gifts that a congregation needs for its growth are rarely to be found in one individual. That is particularly true in such an innovative church as Antioch. It soon became apparent to Barnabas that these new Gentile Christians needed Bible teaching. There were problems of theological understanding arising which he was not adequate to handle. Many of them had little or no knowledge of the Old Testament, so the vocabulary of the Christian gospel, which had been developed in Jerusalem, did not make sense to them. There is an example of that in the telling observation: 'The disciples were first called Christians at Antioch' (11:26).

The word *Christos* is the Greek equivalent of the Hebrew 'Messiah' or 'anointed one'. Every Jew as a result of his synagogue education knew this. *Christos* was not a name, but a title. To speak of '*Christ* Jesus' is a bit like speaking of '*Queen* Elizabeth', or '*President* Bush'. But many Greeks in Antioch were completely ignorant of that Old Testament background; the word to them sounded like Jesus' surname; Jesus Christos. And that is probably how the disciples came to be called Christians in Antioch. It was born out of the confusion of Greek converts concerning the name of their Master. And that, you can be sure, was just the tip of a great iceberg of potential misunderstanding which Barnabas foresaw.

Take a phrase like 'the kingdom of God', for instance. When Jesus had walked the earth he had used it frequently, because he was talking to Jews who knew what it meant. They were immersed in the expectation of a messianic kingdom. But the phrase meant nothing to a Greek. In fact, reference to 'a kingdom' was open to all kinds of political misunderstanding in the Roman world. Christians then would have to find new vocabulary to evangelise Gentiles, or else all kinds of distortions and misunderstandings were going to occur.

175

A classic example, in fact, occurred when Paul was preaching at Athens. We are told he was preaching 'Jesus and the resurrection', but somehow the philosophers of Athens got hold of the idea that he was talking about two divinities; Jesus, and his female consort, Anastasis, the resurrection. Being polytheists they naturally assumed Paul was one also, and they interpreted his words through that cognitive grid.

Any church which is going to make a contribution to missionary advance into unreached cultures must have highly creative and shrewd theologians at its service, who can take the apostolic doctrine of the New Testament and contextualise it into words and ideas that can be assimilated by people whose culture is completely alien to the Bible. That is no simple task, for it is all too easy, in your enthusiasm to help a non-Christian to understand the gospel, to compromise the gospel by fusing it with their existing non-Christian ideas in such a way that it is adulterated. Technically, this is called syncretism and it has happened again and again in church history. One can still observe disastrous examples of it in Latin America today, where catholic ceremony and pagan superstition are frequently so interwoven in the popular mind as to be indistinguishable.

Barnabas, then, had to find somebody with the theological genius to avoid that peril; a theologian who could overcome barriers of cultural misunderstanding in the Gentile world without sacrificing the essential message of the apostolic gospel in the process. Fortunately, he knew just the man for the job. Saul, the brilliant intellectual who had been such an outstanding scholar in the University of Jerusalem before his conversion on the Damascus Road. He was living now, it seems, in some seclusion back in his home town. Barnabas knew he was precisely the person required, because he belonged to two worlds. On the one hand he was a Pharisee, steeped in Bible knowledge, but on the other he was a Roman citizen, eloquent in Greek and totally familiar with secular culture, having been brought up in Tarsus. Barnabas also knew as a result of earlier acquaintance that this man had a special sense of vocation from God and had been marked out as God's chosen instrument for the work of Gentile evangelism. So if anybody was equipped to lick these Greek Christians into theological shape, Saul was. Thus, Barnabas the encouraging pastor became Barnabas the talent-spotter. Off he went to head-hunt the man for the task.

There is a lesson here, for one of the problems we have these days is that we have allowed theology to become part of the university curriculum. The result is that theologians have become career academics, often pursuing their own intellectual interests with little regard for the needs of the Christian community or of Christian mission. Not infrequently in the last hundred years, theologians have hindered and undermined the Christian faith rather than defended and advanced it. It would have been much healthier had the title 'theologian' been reserved for those whom *the church* sets apart for the task of interpreting and teaching biblical truth.

Had scholars understood their role in that church-based way, we would have been spared a great deal. There would have been less theological jargon, for a start; for the true purpose of theology is not to talk about Christianity in vocabulary which is accessible only to academics, but to teach the church how to talk about Christianity in a way that is comprehensible to secular culture. There would also have been fewer futile debates. It is said that when Constantinople was being sacked by the forces of Islam, the theologians of the Eastern church were busy having a debate about how many angels could sit on the tip of a pin! Such an item would not have found its way onto Paul's agenda at Antioch.

If we had kept the missionary purpose of theology paramount, I believe we would also have attracted a higher calibre of Christian into theological study. For I am afraid that all too often young zealous Christians, who are concerned for evangelism, see theology as a dusty irrelevance. Being activists, they want to do something that counts, and as far as they can see, theology does not count for anything. But the truth is that we cannot win the world without missionary theologians. We need men like Paul to teach us how to relate the biblical gospel to other cultures, other philosophies, other languages, and yet remain faithful to its truth. Perhaps every pastor should be like Barnabas, talent-spotting, digging those potential missionary theologians out of their university libraries and putting them where they ought to be: in the frontline of missionary endeavour for the church.

A heart for fellowship

During this time some prophets came down from Jerusalem to Antioch. One of them, named Agabus, stood up and through the Spirit predicted that a severe famine would spread over the entire Roman world. (This happened during the reign of Claudius.) The disciples, each according to his ability, decided to provide help for the brothers living in Judea. This they did, sending their gift to the elders by Barnabas and Saul (11:27–30).

You will remember how from the start the Christians in Jerusalem had demonstrated extraordinary generosity to those in material need, surrendering their goods to the common purse so that the poor could be cared for. The first time we hear of Barnabas, in fact, is in that connection. It is recorded that he sold a field and donated the proceeds to the church for its welfare programme (4:36–37). He taught that same priority clearly to the church at Antioch. And they developed it in a new and important direction. Here, in these verses, we see *inter-church* welfare provision for the first time. More than that, we see a *Gentile* church helping a *Jewish* church.

Could there be any greater testimony to the success of Barnabas and Paul's teaching ministry than this? A Hellenistic congregation, 300 miles from Jerusalem, in a different Roman province, and with a decidedly anti-Semitic background, is so concerned for their Jewish fellow Christians that they make a voluntary collection for their relief from a famine which has not yet even begun. And what a mark of respect that they should delegate not one, but both of their senior ministers to bear the gift to Jerusalem on their behalf. We know from later events that there was a certain suspicion of this Gentile church in Antioch among some in Jerusalem. It may very well be that one of the reasons Barnabas and Saul were keen to take this donation was in order to talk to the apostles about the danger of a Jewish/Gentile rift in the missionary programme. If so, what a disarming gesture it must have been that these Gentiles should show such practical love to their Jewish brothers. It must have impressed the conservative reactionaries in Jerusalem and gone a long way to allay their fears of Gentile evangelism.

Clearly, Antioch, for all its avant-garde image and pioneering theology, was a church which felt itself in partnership with all other churches. It did not wish to compete with Jerusalem or to make itself the capital of its own Christian empire. It saw itself as the local expression of the body of Christ in Antioch, just as the Jerusalem church was the local expression of the body of Christ there. Such an understanding is a vital element if any church is going to have missionary vision. All too often strong churches with busy and successful programmes of local evangelism become self-absorbed and lose interest in what God is doing in other parts of the world. An isolationist mentality settles in, and as their budget grows, a higher and higher proportion of it is spent on their own internal programmes and interests. Sometimes such churches allow themselves to grow without any regard to the effect of their growth on other congregations nearby, and without any sense of responsibility to share the resources their growth has given them. Some may even take pride in the fact that they are doing so much better than another fellowship on the other side of town. And if such churches embark on mission at all, they frequently display precisely the same disregard for the church overseas that they have for other churches at home. There is no thought of collaboration; no investigation of what other Christians might be doing or what other congregations might exist in the places to which they are sending their missionaries. The damage that has been done by this kind of insensitivity over the years is enormous and derives fundamentally from the lack of a real heart for inter-church fellowship.

Antioch, mercifully, suffered no such blind spot, as this generous demonstration of material care for their brothers in Jerusalem clearly shows. A church that is going to have a missionary vision must also be concerned for Christian unity among those who share its gospel and desire to preach it. Those 1.3 billion are never going to be reached by isolationist congregations doing their own thing. It is only as Christians pool their resources and help one another that the Great Commission can be fulfilled.

A praying leadership

> In the church at Antioch there were prophets and teachers: Barnabas, Simeon called Niger, Lucius of Cyrene, Manaen...and Saul. While they were worshipping the Lord and fasting, the Holy Spirit said, 'Set apart for me Barnabas and Saul for the work to which I have called them.' So after they had fasted and prayed, they placed their hands on them and sent them off (13:1–3).

So we at last arrive at the most important step of all.

Evangelistic expansion had been going on under the providential hand of God, but up till now there had been no conscious policy of missionary advance on the part of the Christians. It had been persecution, rather than planning, that had driven the church out to new places, and often it had been pioneering individuals like Philip, rather than whole churches, who had taken the missionary initiative. Now, for the first time, an entire congregation was seeking to push the frontier of the 'unreached' world back by a deliberate step of missionary enterprise.

There are two slightly different ways of interpreting these verses, depending on to whom you think that the pronoun 'they' refers (13:2). Some say that 'they' who were fasting and praying were the entire church at Antioch, and on this view the list of 'prophets and teachers' represents the personnel they were praying about—the short-list of those available for overseas service. It seems more natural though to regard the 'they' as referring to the five men themselves. In which case these were the spiritual leaders of the congregation. It was as a result of their fasting and prayer that the conviction that God was calling the church to send out missionaries derived.

Whichever way you take it, there are several things worthy of note. First, what a mixed bag these prophets and teachers were! Barnabas we know about, he was a priestly Jew; Simeon, though he had a Jewish name, was probably a proselyte because his Latin nickname 'Niger' suggests that he was a negro. He could even have been Simon of Cyrene, the man who carried Jesus' cross. Certainly his colleague Lucius was from Cyrene in North Africa, so he may well have been black too. Then there was Manaen, foster-brother to Herod Antipas who executed John the Baptist. (Is it not an ironic testimony to the grace of God that although these two men were brought up in the same family circle, one of them should become an unscrupulous politician, who contributed to the execution of Christ, and the other should find himself a church leader?) And finally there was Saul, the Pharisee turned Christian. An extraordinary company, yet there can be no doubt that they were brought together in the providence of God, because they all had one thing in common. They were all open-minded about the possibility of Gentile evangelism. It is quite possible in fact that Simeon and Lucius were among the first group of disciples 'from Cyprus and Cyrene' who had come up from Jerusalem after the dispersion, and initiated the programme of Gentile evangelism at Antioch in the first place.

The message this group received from the Holy Spirit as they fasted and prayed, probably given by prophetic utterance, would have been no surprise to them, then. For they must have been thinking in this direction for a long while. Yet you will notice they did not impetuously rush out upon their missionary enterprise. They waited until they were convinced that their vision for mission was also the mind of the Holy Spirit. This missionary initiative derived not from the church, nor even from the church leaders, but from God through the Holy Spirit. Here was a team of church leaders who did not spend all their time organising things, but who sought God's face with a degree of real commitment, because they wanted to pursue the missionary task *his* way.

Notice too whom the Holy Spirit eventually set apart; Barnabas and Saul. These were the two teachers who had built up the church in Antioch. If God had required one of them it would have been sacrifice enough, but both of them! Clearly this church did not believe, then, that the missionfield is a scrap heap for drop-outs from Bible college, or pastors who cannot stand the strain. God uses his best people in this kind of work, and the church must be prepared to make costly sacrifices as a result.

Notice also the way in which the leadership and

the church identify with these missionaries when they eventually set out: 'After they had fasted and prayed, they placed their hands on them and sent them off' (13:3).

It is important to stress that though this was a vital new step into deliberate missionary enterprise, it is only one particular example of such evangelism. There is nothing to suggest that the Holy Spirit will necessarily always lead in precisely this way. Local churches are not always so fortunate as to have a team of prophets and teachers to lead them. On many occasions in church history, progress in Christian mission has taken place in spite of the conservatism and the reluctance of church leaders, rather than because of their dynamic and visionary initiative. Sometimes an individual like William Carey has had to step out completely unsupported by the people of God at large. And sometimes para-church organisations have had to be set up in order to carry the work of mission forward, because the church itself has been negligent or even apostate. We must beware of idealism about the local church's role in the matter. Antiochs are few and far between.

Nevertheless, there are important principles here. One is that Barnabas and Saul did not act independently but consulted with other senior men whom they respected. The missionary call was not an ego trip as far as they were concerned: it was supported by the recognition of others. Too many Christians today ignore this principle and are simply 'doing their own thing' as freelance evangelists without proper accountability.

Secondly, the church itself did not sit around idly waiting for Barnabas and Saul to 'feel led'. It is clear that either the church or its leaders got together, prayed about the matter and, in obedience to the Holy Spirit, approached Barnabas and Saul. Far too many churches are *re*active rather than *pro*active in finding missionary candidates. They wait for others to 'hear the call' instead of being willing to suggest to them that they should be thinking about missionary service. Very often those most suited to the task of mission do not offer themselves readily for service because of a sense of inadequacy or self-depreciation. The church has a responsibility not to wait until such people solicit its support, but to have a missionary vision of its own, encouraging potential candidates to further it.

For all the progress made in the last 2,000 years, that boundary we pointed out at the beginning of the chapter between the 'reached' and 'unreached' is still there. Every day 368,000 new people are born (that is 138 million people a year). So, like the Red Queen in *Alice in Wonderland*, we have to run as hard as we can to stand still in the business of world mission. If we want to make progress, we have to run at least twice as fast as that.

Lord Shaftesbury, the leading evangelical and social reformer, attended a great conference on mission 130 years ago in Liverpool. By the end of the conference he was getting thoroughly frustrated by the prevarication and the hesitation he observed among the Christians there, so he gave a great speech which included this statement: 'Those who hold the truth have means enough, knowledge enough, opportunity enough to evangelise the globe fifty times over.'

I do not know on what statistical analysis he based that judgement. It sounds to me more like oratory than research. But it nevertheless epitomises the challenge the church must face. The task of mission is formidable and it is unfinished. Do we believe it can be finished, or are we defeated at the mere thought of those 1.3 billion 'unreached' people? There is no need to be, for many who study this problem today are confident that if we were sufficiently serious-minded it is perfectly possible to anticipate the Christian penetration of every people group on the face of the earth, even before the end of the twentieth century. We must not be naïve, however, about what such an ambition would demand of us. There is no way those 'unreached' peoples can cross the boundary into the 'reached' category without missionary initiative of the type Antioch undertook on a very large scale, and often in new and imaginative ways. And I think we have to face the fact that at the moment, most of the churches in the West do not have the vision for it. Consider the current distribution of resources. Of all Christian manpower and funds, 99% is consumed at the moment by the churches themselves for their own self-indulgent purposes. Four million full-time workers serve existing congregations compared to the handful who are dedicated to trying to plant new churches among the 'unreached' peoples of the world.

The cause is not hopeless, for there are many zealous young believers, our contemporary equivalent of the men of Cyrene and Cyprus, who have the evangelistic zeal to break through cultural barriers. We have many gifted pastors and theologians like Barnabas and Saul, who could be released for work overseas and provide enormous encouragement to the dynamic new churches in Latin America, Africa and East Asia. Their Bible teaching will be desperately needed in such churches if they are to be equipped with the missionary vision and the theological creativity they will need to advance the leading edge of those ever-increasing circles. And there is a better spirit of interchurch co-operation in evangelism today than ever before. But the unfinished missionary task will not be completed by a better allocation of resources alone. There must surely be a new sense of divine commissioning as well; the Holy Spirit must impress upon us with new urgency our responsibility to take positive steps in reaching the 'unreached'. And we shall discover that as the leaders at Antioch discovered it—not when we are busy planning, but when we are busy praying.

Reached Peoples

500 million
committed Christians

1,200 million
nominal Christians

2,100 million
non-Christians
"within reach"

— — — — — — — — — — — — —

BOUNDARY OF
CHRISTIAN INFLUENCE
IN 1991

Unreached Peoples

1,300 million
"unreached"
non-Christians

including: 650 people-groups
80 mega-cities